From the book

RTI

Phonological Awareness Interventions
for the Regular Classroom Teacher

RTI Intervention Focus:

Rhyming and Word Families

Second Edition

Dr. Sherri Dobbs Santos

ISBN# 978-0-578-02817-0

Special thanks to Janice Miller for her second pair of eyes and her meticulous editing of this book.

Cover Design by artist Richard Dobbs Jr.
See more of his work at:
www.dobbsart.com

RICHARD DOBBS
PAINTINGS, MURALS, & ILLUSTRATIONS

Books by Dr. Sherri Dobbs Santos:

RTI: Speech and Language Interventions for the Regular Classroom Teacher

RTI: Phonological Awareness Interventions for the Regular Classroom Teacher

RTI Intervention Focus: Letter Recognition

RTI Intervention Focus: Letter Sounds

RTI Intervention Focus: Rhyming and Word Families

RTI Intervention Focus: Word Parts and Segmenting

RTI Intervention Focus: Blending

RTI Intervention Focus: Sight Word Recognition

RTI Intervention Focus: Number Recognition

I DO – WE DO – YOU DO: An RTI Intervention for Math Problem Solving Grades 1-5

Benjamin Franklin Biography and Plays

Thomas Jefferson Biography and Plays

Lewis and Clark Biography and Plays

Sacagawea Biography and Plays

Mavis Davis Unlocks the Past

RTI YOU CAN DO!
rtiyoucando.com

All books available for purchase at www.rtiyoucando.com **or at** http://www.lulu.com/spotlight/sherrisantos.
Contact Dr. Sherri Dobbs Santos at: rti@rtiyoucando.com

Table of Contents

INTRODUCTION

When the RTI model was introduced in my school district in 2007, I thought, here we go again; a new program, new ideas, and a whole new set of acronyms to remember. By the time RTI came around, I was no longer teaching in the regular classroom. I had been promoted to the position of Student Support Specialist (SSS) and was to coordinate the Student Support Team (SST) process at two elementary schools in Henry County, Georgia. Among my duties as the SSS, I was to assist teachers with students experiencing difficulties in the classroom, whether it was for academic reasons, behavior concerns, attention issues, speech difficulties, problems with fine motor coordination, etc. I was to coordinate meetings with parents, give students screening evaluations, and provide teachers with the support and materials needed to help their at-risk students. I was also the person who facilitated the process of referring students for special education testing. I was responsible for collecting the evidence necessary to make a referral for testing which, in many cases, led to placement into special education classes. I became quite proficient at establishing procedures, rules, and guidelines and my teachers were trying their best to provide individualized interventions for their students at the different tiers outlined in the RTI model. They were willing to try new techniques and were doing their best to document what they were doing. However, despite the time I spent researching best practices and reading up on the latest research to share with them they were struggling, and I felt their frustrations. I had created "intervention sheets" for my teachers which cited the research and gave a general idea of how to implement an RTI intervention with a student. Yet, despite my best efforts, my teachers were **still** struggling. When listening to their concerns about RTI, it became clear to me that they needed something more specific. They wanted something that was easy-to-implement, structured, and actually helped the student. They were begging for specific lessons and a guide to help them through the RTI process. They didn't want to have to spend extra hours searching for materials or researching how to implement interventions. They also didn't want to spend extra time creating assessments to evaluate students throughout the intervention process. My teachers were looking to me for answers and I was under pressure to give them the solutions they were desperately searching for. That's when I started thinking about creating an intervention format that was easy-to-follow, contained lessons that were both based on the latest research, and also provided the baseline and data point assessments necessary for progress monitoring. I began with the U.S. Department of Education Institute of Education Sciences: What Works Clearinghouse website. From the research studies that either met or met with reservations the "What Works Clearinghouse" (WWC) evidence standards in the area of phonological awareness training plus letter knowledge training I created a format of lessons which are user friendly, easy to implement and easy to document. What follows is the compilation of that research.

WHAT IS RTI?

Response to Intervention (RTI) is a multi-tier approach to the early identification and support of students with learning and behavior needs. The RTI process begins with high-quality instruction and universal screening of all children in the general education classroom. Struggling learners are provided with interventions at increasing levels of intensity to accelerate their rate of learning. These services may be provided by a variety of personnel, including general education teachers, special educators, and specialists. Progress is closely monitored to assess both the learning rate and level of performance of individual students. Educational decisions about the intensity and duration of interventions are based on individual student response to instruction. RTI is designed for use when making decisions in both general education and special education, creating a well-integrated system of instruction and intervention guided by child outcome data. (National Center for Learning Disabilities, 2008)

RTI MODEL

Each state has adopted an RTI model through which students receive appropriate interventions based on their individual needs. The diagram below is an example of a four tier model (from the state of Georgia), however, many states have opted for a three tier model. For students suspected of having a Specific Learning Disability, an appropriate intervention **must** be implemented for a minimum of twelve academic weeks. Monitoring of the student's progress throughout the intervention **must** occur. A baseline assessment **must** be given before the intervention begins and at least four data points (assessments) **must** be taken throughout the twelve week period (approximately once every three weeks). Decisions for new interventions, psychological testing, special education testing or placement, etc. should be based on the data collected throughout the twelve week intervention and should be made in the context of a committee that includes the teacher, the student's parents, administrators, counselors, and/or other highly qualified educational personnel. The student's RTI should be assessed by looking at how much progress was made overall **and** where the student is functioning in relation to the standards set forth by the state and/or district. Students who make significant progress but who are still functioning below grade level may simply need more time with the current intervention to catch up. **Just because a student is below grade level does not mean he/she is a candidate for special education.** The RTI process is individualized and rash decisions concerning a student's placement should be avoided at all costs.

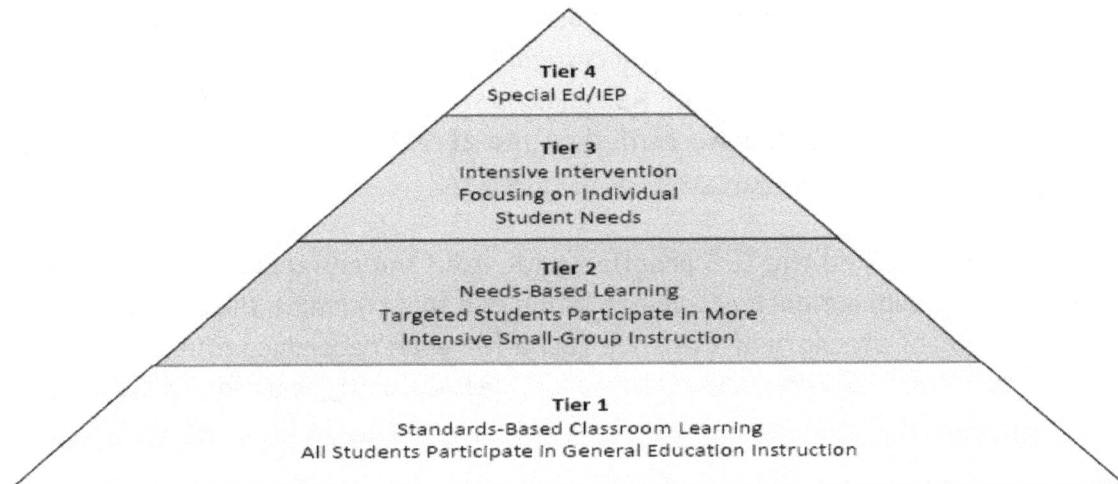

Tier 4
Special Ed/IEP

Tier 3
Intensive Intervention
Focusing on Individual
Student Needs

Tier 2
Needs-Based Learning
Targeted Students Participate in More
Intensive Small-Group Instruction

Tier 1
Standards-Based Classroom Learning
All Students Participate in General Education Instruction

EVIDENCE BASED

The intervention in this manual was developed and designed using the **strongest** of five recommendations cited in the following report:

Gersten, R., Compton, D., Connor, C.M., Dimino, J., Santoro, L., Linan-Thompson, S., and Tilly, W.D. (2008). Assisting students struggling with reading: Response to Intervention and multi-tier intervention for reading in the primary grades. A practice guide. (NCEE 2009-4045). Washington, DC: National Center for Education Evaluation and Regional Assistance, Institute of Education Sciences, U.S. Department of Education. Retrieved from http://ies.ed.gov/ncee/wwc/publications/practiceguides/.

This report is available on the IES website at http://ies.ed.gov/ncee and http://ies.ed.gov/ncee/wwc/publications/practiceguides/.

The Institute of Education Sciences (IES) publishes practice guides in education to bring the best available evidence and expertise to bear on the types of systemic challenges that cannot currently be addressed by single interventions or programs. Authors of practice guides seldom conduct the types of systematic literature searches that are the backbone of a meta-analysis, although they take advantage of such work when it is already published. Instead, authors use their expertise to identify the most important research with respect to their recommendations, augmented by a search of recent publications to ensure that research citations are up-to-date. Unique to IES-sponsored practice guides is that they are subjected to rigorous external peer review through the same office that is responsible for independent review of other IES publications. A critical task for peer reviewers of a practice guide is to determine whether the evidence cited in support of particular recommendations is up-to-date and that studies of similar or better quality that point in a different direction have not been ignored. Because practice guides depend on the expertise of their authors and their group decision-making, the content of a practice guide is not and should not be viewed as a set of recommendations that in every case depends on and flows inevitably from scientific research. The goal of this practice guide is to formulate specific and coherent evidence-based recommendations for use by educators addressing the challenge of reducing the number of children who fail to learn how to read proficiently by using "response to intervention" as a means of both preventing reading difficulty and identifying students who need more help. This is called Response to Intervention (RtI). The guide provides practical, clear information on critical RtI topics and is based on the best available evidence as judged by the panel. Recommendations in this guide should not be construed to imply that no further research is warranted on the effectiveness of particular RtI strategies. http://ies.ed.gov/ncee/wwc/publications/practiceguides/.

The expert panel that authored the IES practice guide used the criteria established by the What Works Clearinghouse to support each recommendation and to determine the level of evidence found to back them up. The level of strength of evidence found for each recommendation is explained on the following page: http://ies.ed.gov/ncee/wwc/pdf/practiceguides/rti_reading_pg_021809.pdf

Strong: refers to consistent and generalizable evidence that an intervention program causes better outcomes.

Moderate: refers to evidence from studies that allow strong causal conclusions but cannot be generalized with assurance to the population on which a recommendation is focused (perhaps because the findings have not been widely replicated) or to evidence from studies that are generalizable but have more causal ambiguity than offered by experimental designs (such as statistical models of correlational data or group comparison designs for which equivalence of the groups at pretest is uncertain).

Low: refers to expert opinion based on reasonable extrapolations from research and theory on other topics and evidence from studies that do not meet the standards for moderate or strong evidence. The Table below shows the panel's recommendations and corresponding levels of evidence

Recommendation	Level of evidence
1. Screen all students for potential reading problems at the beginning of the year and again in the middle of the year. Regularly monitor the progress of students at risk for developing reading disabilities.	Moderate
Tier 1 intervention/general education	
2. Provide time for differentiated reading instruction for all students based on assessments of students' current reading level.	Low
Tier 2 intervention	
3. Provide intensive, systematic instruction on up to three foundational reading skills in small groups to students who score below the benchmark score on universal screening. Typically, these groups meet between three and five times a week, for 20 to 40 minutes.	**Strong**
4. Monitor the progress of tier 2 students at least once a month. Use these data to determine whether students still require intervention. For those students still making insufficient progress, school wide teams should design a tier 3 intervention plan.	Low
Tier 3 intervention	
5. Provide intensive instruction on a daily basis that promotes the development of the various components of reading proficiency to students who show minimal progress after reasonable time in tier 2 small group instruction (tier 3).	Low

http://ies.ed.gov/ncee/wwc/pdf/practiceguides/rti_reading_pg_021809.pdf

THE INTERVENTION IN THIS BOOK WAS CREATED PRIMARILY USING RECOMMENDATION #3 (see table above) .

RECOMMENDATION #3
Provide intensive, systematic instruction on up to three foundational reading skills in small groups to students who score below the benchmark score on universal screening. Typically, these groups meet between three and five times a week, for 20 to 40 minutes.

The expert panel stated:
Tier 2 instruction should take place in small homogenous groups ranging from three to four students using curricula that address the major components of reading instruction (comprehension, fluency, phonemic awareness, phonics, and vocabulary). The areas of instruction are based on the results of students' scores on universal screening. Instruction should be

systematic—building skills gradually and introducing skills first in isolation and then integrating them with other skills. Explicit instruction involves more teacher-student interaction, including frequent opportunities for student practice and comprehensible and specific feedback. Intensive instruction should occur three to five times per week for 20 to 40 minutes.

Level of evidence: Strong

The panel judged the evidence supporting this recommendation as strong based on 11 studies that met WWC standards or that met WWC standards with reservations. These studies on supplemental instruction in reading support tier 2 intervention as a way to improve reading performance in decoding. Six studies showed positive effects on decoding, and four showed effects on both decoding and reading comprehension. Six studies involved one-on-one instruction, and the remainder used small groups ranging from two to five students. Given that effect sizes were not significantly higher for the one-on-one approach, small group work could be considered more practical for implementation.

The following are the research citations for the 11 studies noted on the previous page:

Ebaugh, J. C. (2000). The effects of fluency instruction on the literacy development of at-risk first graders. (Doctoral dissertation, Fordham University, 2000). Dissertation Abstracts International, 61(06A), 0072

Ehri, L. C., Dreyer, L. G., Flugman, B., & Gross, A. (2007). Reading rescue: An effective tutoring intervention model for language-minority students who are struggling readers in first grade. American Educational Research Journal, 44(2), 414–48.

Gibbs, S. E. L. (2001). Effects of a one-to-one phonological awareness intervention on first grade students identified as at risk for the acquisition of beginning reading. (Doctoral dissertation, University of South Carolina, 2001). Dissertation Abstracts International, 62(07A), 0202.

Gunn, B., Biglan, A., Smolkowski, K., & Ary, D. (2000). The efficacy of supplemental instruction in decoding skills for Hispanic and non-Hispanic students in early elementary school. The Journal of Special Education, 34(2), 90-103.

Jenkins, J. R., Peyton, J. A., Sanders, E. A., & Vadasy, P. F. (2004). Effects of reading decodable texts in supplemental first-grade tutoring. Scientific Studies of Reading, 8(1), 53-85.

Lennon, J. E., & Slesinski, C. (1999). Early intervention in reading: Results of a screening and intervention program for kindergarten students. School Psychology Review, 28(3), 353-364.

Mathes, P. G., Denton, C., Fletcher, J., Anthony, J., Francis, D., & Schatschneider, C. (2005). The effects of theoretically different instruction and student characteristics on the skills of struggling readers. Reading Research Quarterly, 40(2), 148-182.

McMaster, K. L., Fuchs, D., Fuchs, L. S., & Compton, D. L. (2005). Responding to nonresponders: An experimental field trial of identification and intervention methods. Exceptional Children, 71(4), 445–463.

Vadasy, P. F., Jenkins, J. R., Antil, L. R., Wayne, S. K., & O'Connor, R. E. (1997). The effectiveness of one-to-one tutoring by community tutors for at-risk beginning readers. Learning Disability Quarterly, 20(2), 126–139.

Vadasy, P. F., Sanders, E. A., & Peyton, J. A. (2005). Relative effectiveness of reading practice or word-level instruction in supplemental tutoring: How text matters. Journal of Learning Disabilities, 38(4), 364–380.

Vaughn, S., & Fuchs, L.S. (2006). A response to "Competing views: A dialogue on response to intervention." Assessment for Effective Intervention, 32(1), 58–61.

DELIVERY METHOD:

The intervention in this book is most conducive to one-on-one instruction in which the teacher/tutor works individually with the student. However, this intervention can also be implemented with a small group of two to four students. If a small group approach is used, be sure that every student in the group has his/her own set of instructional cards (if needed for that session).

HOW TO USE THIS MANUAL:

This manual is designed to give teachers the tools necessary to implement an evidence-based intervention for students struggling with blending sounds to read words. The lessons walk the teacher, tutor, or interventionist through the steps of implementation and provide him/her with an easy-to- administer short assessment which tells if the student is ready to move on to the next lesson or if re-teaching is necessary. **TEACHING TO MASTERY** is the goal. The student sets the pace and may spend differing amounts of time on different lessons. This manual also supplies the teacher, tutor, or interventionist with the documents needed for universal screening/baseline and data point assessments and for the graphing of the student's response to the intervention (RTI).

RHYMING AND WORD FAMILIES OVERVIEW

Once it is determined that a student needs this intervention (as evidenced on the **Universal Screening: Rhyming and Word Families Assessment**), make a copy of the appropriate pages (listed on the "Rhyming and Word Families Let's Get Started!" page) including the "Rhyming and Word Families Lesson Checklist." Use the checklist to check off when each lesson was taught and when it was mastered. Do not move forward to a new lesson until the student has mastered the lesson he/she is currently on. Also, to assess the student's response to the intervention, be sure to monitor his/her progress weekly throughout the twelve-week implementation period using the Progress Monitoring Assessments (regardless of which lesson he/she is currently working on). If a student completes all of the Rhyming and Word Families lessons within two to six weeks, he/she still needs to be assessed for at least 2 additional weeks past the point of mastery so as to rule out "lucky guesses" or a "fluke" with the assessment showing said mastery, If the student has truly MASTERED the Rhyming and Word Families Intervention before the 12-week intervention period ends (as evidenced by the **Progress Monitoring: Rhyming and Word Families Assessments**), it would be prudent to move on to an intervention which focuses on more complex concepts such as segmenting and word parts or blending. Be sure to collect baseline data before beginning any new intervention.

The mini- assessments that are a part of the individual lessons are NOT to be used as data point assessments or the universal screening/baseline. The purpose of those assessments is to assist the teacher, tutor, or interventionist in knowing whether or not the student has or has not mastered a particular lesson. The overall timeline for the intervention is 12 weeks with at least three 30-minute sessions occurring each week. However, the intervention session lessons in this manual are **not** timed and should be taught in succession. The student sets the pace according to his/her ability to understand and master the material. A student may be able to finish two or three lessons in a twenty or thirty minute time span whereas another student may be able to only complete and master one lesson over a period of three or four days or even weeks. RTI is an individualized process and is strictly geared to meet the individual needs of the student. This book is not intended to replace the regular classroom curriculum and is not comprehensive or exhaustive. The lessons in this manual should be considered supplemental to what is already being taught in the classroom and are geared to help fill the learning gaps of struggling students whose weak phonics skills interfere with their ability to read fluently which then negatively impacts their ability to comprehend written text. This intervention is intended to strengthen skills through intensive exposure to basic phonological concepts and each individual lesson should be taught to mastery. Using sorting, comparing and contrasting activities, repetition, and drill and practice, this intervention can bring success to those who otherwise would continue to fall through the cracks by helping build a strong foundation on which higher levels of learning can occur.

PROGRESS MONITORING

As stated before, in order to ascertain whether or not the Rhyming and Word Families intervention in this manual is effective, data should be gathered on a weekly basis through the progress monitoring assessments. As with the universal screening, the student must complete the progress monitoring assessments without extra prompts or assistance. All progress monitoring assessments can be scored directly on the corresponding recording sheets provided to you in this manual. It is worthy to note that the universal screening/baseline assessments are identical to the weekly progress monitoring assessments in both format and structure. This gives the educator/assessor a simple way to collect data as well as creates a format that is easy to read and analyze. Because of the continuity among the assessments, the educator/assessor will essentially be comparing 'oranges to oranges' which allows for a more accurate picture of how the student is progressing throughout the intervention.

PROGRESS MONITORING DOCUMENTATION, GRAPH, AND DATA ANALYSIS For
the purpose of data analysis for the Rhyming and Word Families intervention, a graph will be needed to record the data from the universal screening/baseline assessment and each progress monitoring assessment. Graphs are an easy-to-read 'snap shot' of how the student performs each week and are an excellent tool to use when looking at overall progress and effectiveness of an intervention. The data should be analyzed weekly rather than at the end of the 12 weeks so that changes or adjustments to the intervention may be made DURING the 12 week period. The graph below is an example of what an RTI intervention graph may look like after the 12th week of the Rhyming and Word Families intervention. Careful examination of the data collected each week must occur (preferably in the context of a data analysis team) in order to adequately assess the effectiveness of the intervention and to pinpoint areas of weakness. This on-going weekly review of the data is crucial and should be the catalyst which drives future instruction for the struggling student.

SAMPLE GRAPH FOR STUDENT 'X':

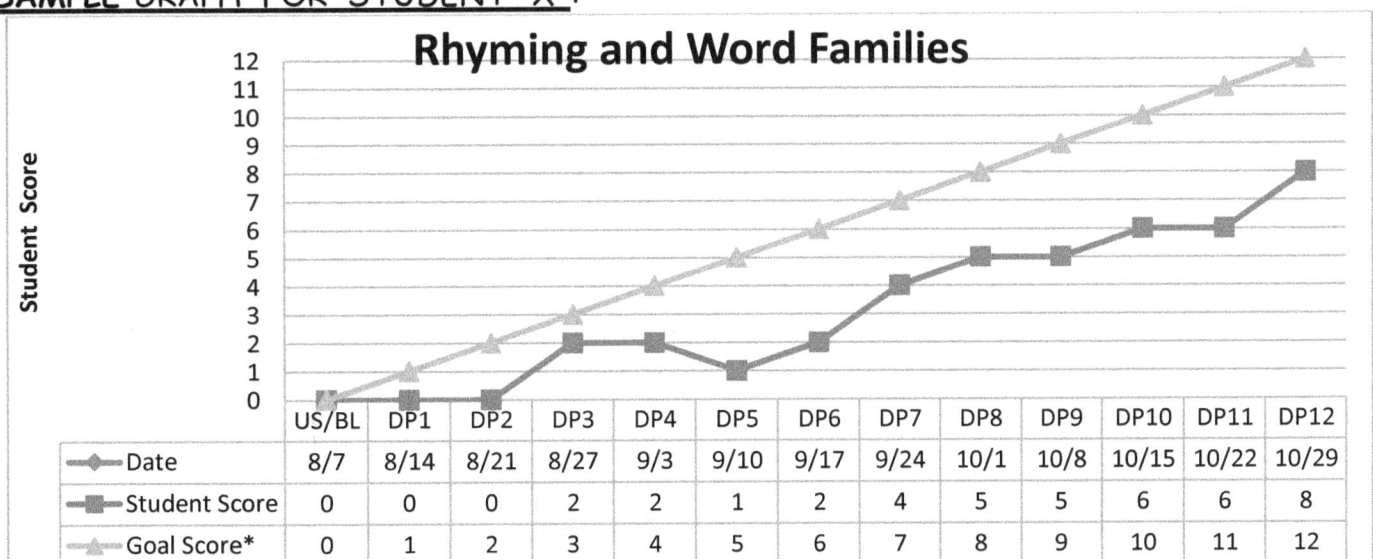

Rhyming and Word Families

	US/BL	DP1	DP2	DP3	DP4	DP5	DP6	DP7	DP8	DP9	DP10	DP11	DP12
Date	8/7	8/14	8/21	8/27	9/3	9/10	9/17	9/24	10/1	10/8	10/15	10/22	10/29
Student Score	0	0	0	2	2	1	2	4	5	5	6	6	8
Goal Score*	0	1	2	3	4	5	6	7	8	9	10	11	12

What does the sample graph on the previous page tell us about Student 'X'? According to the universal screening/baseline assessment (given 8-7-11) the student scored a 0 out of a possible 12 signifying he/she lacks the ability to hear rhymes, say rhymes, or identify word families. After 12 weeks of the rhyming and word families intervention, Student 'X' has made progress but has yet to reach his/her goal score. Twice the scores remained the same and a regression in scores was noted between DP4 and DP5. However, Student 'X's growth line overall steadily increased. At the end of the 12th week of intervention, Student 'X' has consistently fallen short of the weekly goals but is showing gains overall. Additional time with the same intervention would be the logical recommendation for this student until mastery has been achieved.

Let's Get Started!

To implement the Rhyming and Word Families intervention in this manual, copy the following pages for each student in the intervention group:

- *Universal Screening Teacher Recording Sheet (p. 14)*
- *Progress Monitoring Teacher Recording Sheets (pp. 15-17)*
- *Universal Screening & Progress Monitoring RTI Graph (p. 18)*
- *Rhyming and Word Families Lessons Checklist (pp. 19-20)*
- *Rhyming and Word Families Mini-Assessments (pp. 21-26)*
- *Word Family Cards (pp. 63-81)*

Universal Screening Teacher Recording Sheet
Rhyming and Word Families

Student Name: _____ Grade: _____ Teacher: _____ Date: _____

Section A. Hearing Rhymes: Have the student sit facing you and explain that you will say two words. Tell him/her to say "YES" if the two words rhyme and "NO" if they do not. Have student practice this skill using the words 'book/look' and 'dirt/cup'. Explain that the words 'book/look' rhyme because their ending sounds are the same whereas 'dirt/cup' do not because their ending sounds are different.

Word Pair	YES	NO	Word Pair	YES	NO	Word Pair	YES	NO	Word Pair	YES	NO
pig/wig			hot/spot			dog/dark			red/bread		

Section B. Saying Rhymes: Have the student sit facing you and explain that you will say one word and that he/she will say a second word that rhymes with your word. Have the student practice this skill by stating the following: "Say a word that rhymes with 'mouse'." If the student gives a correct response then proceed with this evaluation. If the student does not give a correct response, then briefly explain that rhyming words have the same ending sounds. Explain that 'house' rhymes with 'mouse' because their ending sounds are the same. Once the student understands, proceed with this evaluation.

Word	Response	Word	Response	Word	Response	Word	Response
bid		tad		fun		sat	

Section C. Identifying Word Families: Explain to the student that he/she will hear two words from a particular word family and that he/she will say which family they are from. For example, the words 'bend' and 'lend' are from the -end family.

Word Pair	Response	Word Pair	Response	Word Pair	Response	Word Pair	Response
mop/top	(-op)	fan/tan	(-an)	bump/stump	(-ump)	gong/long	(-ong)

Total # Correct _____ (Total # Possible = 12)

Progress Monitoring Teacher Recording Sheet
Rhyming and Word Families

Student Name: _____ Grade: _____ Teacher: _____

Refer to the directions from the Universal Screening assessment to complete each data point assessment.

Data Point 1
Date: _____

Hearing Rhymes: Total Correct (out of a total of 12): _____

Word Pair	YES	NO	Word Pair	YES	NO	Word Pair	YES	NO	Word Pair	YES	NO
wag/lag			sunk/sold			lift/gift			net/wet		

Saying Rhymes:

Word	Response	Word	Response	Word	Response	Word	Response
nod		tank		moon		belt	

Identifying Word Families:

Word Pair	Response	Word Pair	Response	Word Pair	Response	Word Pair	Response
torch/scorch	*(-orch)*	spice/dice	*(-ice)*	bump/stump	*(-ump)*	gong/long	*(-ong)*

Data Point 2
Date: _____

Hearing Rhymes: Total Correct (out of a total of 12): _____

Word Pair	YES	NO	Word Pair	YES	NO	Word Pair	YES	NO	Word Pair	YES	NO
more/mud			hung/lung			help/hope			rub/tub		

Saying Rhymes:

Word	Response	Word	Response	Word	Response	Word	Response
bid		tad		fun		sat	

Identifying Word Families:

Word Pair	Response	Word Pair	Response	Word Pair	Response	Word Pair	Response
sort/snort	*(-ort)*	cart/smart	*(-art)*	reach/beach	*(-each)*	cake/bake	*(-ake)*

Data Point 3
Date: _____

Hearing Rhymes: Total Correct (out of a total of 12): _____

Word Pair	YES	NO	Word Pair	YES	NO	Word Pair	YES	NO	Word Pair	YES	NO
chair/fair			ground/mound			felt/fast			palm/bug		

Saying Rhymes:

Word	Response	Word	Response	Word	Response	Word	Response
hand		corn		rub		trip	

Identifying Word Families:

Word Pair	Response	Word Pair	Response	Word Pair	Response	Word Pair	Response
sun/run	*(-un)*	shook/book	*(-ook)*	bike/like	*(-ike)*	vet/pet	*(-et)*

Data Point 4
Date: _____

Hearing Rhymes: Total Correct (out of a total of 12): _____

Word Pair	YES	NO	Word Pair	YES	NO	Word Pair	YES	NO	Word Pair	YES	NO
rot/rat			light/fight			pint/beg			tuck/duck		

Saying Rhymes:

Word	Response	Word	Response	Word	Response	Word	Response
mad		hen		pink		grade	

Identifying Word Families:

Word Pair	Response	Word Pair	Response	Word Pair	Response	Word Pair	Response
quack/black	*(-ack)*	fit/hit	*(-it)*	stamp/ramp	*(-amp)*	seal/deal	*(-eal)*

Student Name: _____ Grade: _____ Teacher: _____

Refer to the directions from the Universal Screening assessment to complete each data point assessment

Data Point 5   Date: _____

Hearing Rhymes: Total Correct (out of a total of 12): _____

Word Pair	YES	NO	Word Pair	YES	NO	Word Pair	YES	NO	Word Pair	YES	NO
med/fed			hug/bug			yes/yet			got/boat		

Saying Rhymes:

Word	Response	Word	Response	Word	Response	Word	Response
like		ring		pump		look	

Identifying Word Families:

Word Pair	Response	Word Pair	Response	Word Pair	Response	Word Pair	Response
mole/pole	(-ole)	mold/cold	(-old)	stir/fir	(-ir)	shut/hut	(-ut)

Data Point 6   Date: _____

Hearing Rhymes: Total Correct (out of a total of 12): _____

Word Pair	YES	NO	Word Pair	YES	NO	Word Pair	YES	NO	Word Pair	YES	NO
van/can			rile/mile			tax/fax			good/look		

Saying Rhymes:

Word	Response	Word	Response	Word	Response	Word	Response
bay		hold		fat		brick	

Identifying Word Families:

Word Pair	Response	Word Pair	Response	Word Pair	Response	Word Pair	Response
step/pep	(-ep)	play/day	(-ay)	cloud/loud	(-oud)	rough/tough	(-ough)

Data Point 7   Date: _____

Hearing Rhymes: Total Correct (out of a total of 12): _____

Word Pair	YES	NO	Word Pair	YES	NO	Word Pair	YES	NO	Word Pair	YES	NO
jet/pet			bond/gold			sad/wed			cart/mart		

Saying Rhymes:

Word	Response	Word	Response	Word	Response	Word	Response
hair		vine		lock		jeep	

Identifying Word Families:

Word Pair	Response	Word Pair	Response	Word Pair	Response	Word Pair	Response
dill/bill	(-ill)	star/bar	(-ar)	like/kick	(-ick)	line/mine	(-ine)

Data Point 8   Date: _____

Hearing Rhymes: Total Correct (out of a total of 12): _____

Word Pair	YES	NO	Word Pair	YES	NO	Word Pair	YES	NO	Word Pair	YES	NO
rent/fence			had/fad			nope/hop			lip/lap		

Saying Rhymes:

Word	Response	Word	Response	Word	Response	Word	Response
mat		wish		goat		hog	

Identifying Word Families:

Word Pair	Response	Word Pair	Response	Word Pair	Response	Word Pair	Response
limp/chimp	(-imp)	fringe/hinge	(-inge)	wall/ball	(-all)	frame/name	(-ame)

Student Name: _____ Grade: _____ Teacher: _____

Data Point 9
Date: _____

Hearing Rhymes: Total Correct (out of a total of 12): _____

Word Pair	YES	NO	Word Pair	YES	NO	Word Pair	YES	NO	Word Pair	YES	NO
jump/bump			why/shy			clock/crank			plus/vet		

Saying Rhymes:

Word	Response	Word	Response	Word	Response	Word	Response
mind		time		leaf		tank	

Identifying Word Families:

Word Pair	Response	Word Pair	Response	Word Pair	Response	Word Pair	Response
paw/saw	(-aw)	tick/hick	(-ick)	shade/made	(-ade)	slip/tip	(-ip)

Data Point 10
Date: _____

Hearing Rhymes: Total Correct (out of a total of 12): _____

Word Pair	YES	NO	Word Pair	YES	NO	Word Pair	YES	NO	Word Pair	YES	NO
bid/hid			mud/lot			quit/quick			back/pack		

Saying Rhymes:

Word	Response	Word	Response	Word	Response	Word	Response
truck		sell		pill		sock	

Identifying Word Families:

Word Pair	Response	Word Pair	Response	Word Pair	Response	Word Pair	Response
hen/men	(-en)	vest/best	(-est)	save/shave	(-ave)	glare/bare	(-are)

Data Point 11
Date: _____

Hearing Rhymes: Total Correct (out of a total of 12): _____

Word Pair	YES	NO	Word Pair	YES	NO	Word Pair	YES	NO	Word Pair	YES	NO
hex/vex			till/tame			black/track			kick/fox		

Saying Rhymes:

Word	Response	Word	Response	Word	Response	Word	Response
fuzz		bath		ware		pound	

Identifying Word Families:

Word Pair	Response	Word Pair	Response	Word Pair	Response	Word Pair	Response
stack/hack	(-ack)	heal/meal	(-eal)	mile/vile	(-ile)	page/gage	(-age)

Data Point 12
Date: _____

Hearing Rhymes: Total Correct (out of a total of 12): _____

Word Pair	YES	NO	Word Pair	YES	NO	Word Pair	YES	NO	Word Pair	YES	NO
grape/grade			blue/hue			lot/cot			zoo/zip		

Saying Rhymes:

Word	Response	Word	Response	Word	Response	Word	Response
get		bile		deer		vet	

Identifying Word Families:

Word Pair	Response	Word Pair	Response	Word Pair	Response	Word Pair	Response
maze/haze	(-aze)	duck/luck	(-uck)	face/lace	(-ace)	moon/noon	(-oon)

RTI GRAPH
UNIVERSAL SCREENING & PROGRESS MONITORING
Rhyming and Word Families

Student Name: _____ Grade: _____ Teacher: _____

On the graph below, plot the Universal Screening/Baseline (US/BL) and all data point (DP) scores for each comprehensive rhyming and word families assessment given.

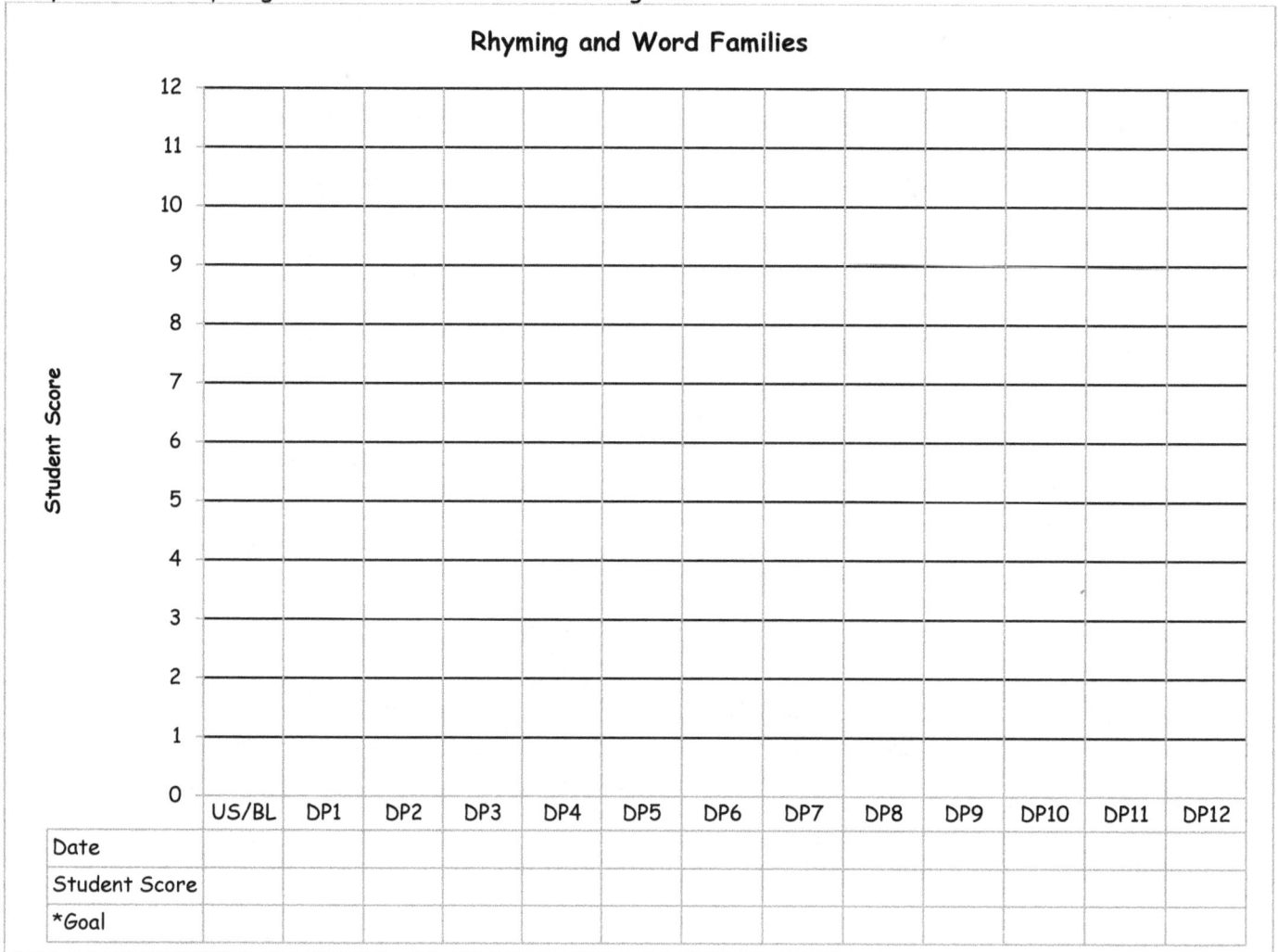

Rhyming and Word Families

Student Score (y-axis: 0–12)

	US/BL	DP1	DP2	DP3	DP4	DP5	DP6	DP7	DP8	DP9	DP10	DP11	DP12
Date													
Student Score													
*Goal													

*Establish goal line before intervention begins

18

Rhyming and Word Families Lesson Checklist

Name of Lesson	Date(s) lesson was taught	Date lesson was mastered
Lesson 1: Hearing Three Letter Words that Rhyme *-at, -ad, -ag*		
Lesson 2: Hearing Three Letter Words that Rhyme *-ed, -en, -et*		
Lesson 3: Hearing Three Letter Words that Rhyme *-ig, -id, -ib*		
Lesson 4: Hearing Three Letter Words that Rhyme *-og, -ot, -od*		
Lesson 5: Hearing Three Letter Words that Rhyme *-ub, -ug, -um*		
Lesson 6: Saying Words that Rhyme *-at, -ad, -ag, -ed, -en, -et, -ig, -id, -ib, -og, -ot, -od, -ub, -ug, -um*		
Lesson 7: Hearing More Words that Rhyme *-all, -alm, -ill, -old, -oll, -ell, -elp, -ull*		
Lesson 8: Hearing More Words that Rhyme *-and, -ang, -ank, -ing, -ink, -int*		
Lesson 9: Hearing More Words that Rhyme *-ond, -ong, -end, -ung, -unk, -ant*		
Lesson 10: Hearing More Words that Rhyme *-art, -ast, -ift, -irt, -ist, -ort*		
Lesson 11: Hearing More Words that Rhyme *-ost, -eft, -elt, -est, -ust, -ass*		
Lesson 12: Hearing More Words that Rhyme *-amp, -iss, -oss, -omp, -ess, -ump*		
Lesson 13: Saying More Words that Rhyme *-all, -alm, -ill, -old, -oll, -ell, -elp, -ull, -and, -ang, -ank, -ing, -ink, -int, -ond, -ong, -end, -ung, -unk, -ant, -art, -ast, -ift, -irt, -ist, -ort, -ost, -eft, -elt, -est, -ust, -ass, -amp, -iss, -oss, -omp, -ess, -ump*		
Lesson 14: Hearing Even More Words that Rhyme *-ash, -ath, -atch, -arch, -ish, -ith*		
Lesson 15: Even More Words that Rhyme *-itch, -irth, -osh, -otch, -oth, -orch*		
Lesson 16: Hearing Long Vowel Rhyming Words *-ace, -ade, -age, -ake, -ale, -ame, -ape*		
Lesson 17: Hearing Long Vowel Rhyming Words *-ate, -ice, -ide, -ife, -ile, -ine, -ite*		

Lesson 18: Hearing Long Vowel Rhyming Words -ive, -ode, -oke, -ole, -one, -ope, -ote		
Lesson 19: Hearing <u>Special</u> Long Vowel Rhyming Words -aid, -ail, -ain, -ait, -ay, -eat, -each		
Lesson 20: Hearing <u>Special</u> Long Vowel Rhyming Words -ead, -eak, -eam, -ean, -eet, -eed, -eek		
Lesson 21: Hearing <u>Special</u> Long Vowel Rhyming Words -eel, -eem, -eep, -oach, -oad, -oam, -oan, oat		
Lesson 22: Saying Even More Words that Rhyme -ash, -ath, -atch, -arch, -ish, -ith, -itch,-irth, -osh, -otch, -oth, -orch, -ace, -ade, -age, -ake, -ale, -ame, -ape, -ate, -ice, -ide, -ife, -ile, -ine, -ite, -ive, -ode, -oke, -ole, -one, -ope, -ote, -aid, -ail, -ain, -ait, -ay, -eat, -each, -ead, -eak, -eam, -ean, -eet, -eed, -eek, -eel, -eem, -eep, -oach, -oad, -oam, -oan, -oat		
Lesson 23: Hearing Special Rhyming Words -oil, -oin, -oint, -oist, -oot, -ook, -oom		
Lesson 24: Hearing Special Rhyming Words -ound, -our, -ouse, -out, -oon, -oop		
Lesson 25: Hearing Special r-Controlled Rhyming Words -ar, -ard, -arm, -arn, -art, -er, -ern		
Lesson 26: Hearing Special r-Controlled Rhyming Words -ird, -irt, -or, -ord, -ork, -orn, -ir, -ur		
Lesson 27: Hearing Special l-Controlled Rhyming Words -ald, -alk, -eld, -elt, -ild, -old		
Lesson 28: Hearing Special w-Controlled Rhyming Words -aw, -awn, -ew, -ow, -own		
Lesson 29: Saying Even More Words that Rhyme -oil, -oin, -oint, -oist, -oot, -ook, -oom, -ound, -our, -ouse, -out, -oon, -oop, -ar, -ard, -arm, -arn,-art, -er, -ern, -ird, -irt, -or, -ord, -ork, -orn, -ir, -ur, -ald, -alk, -eld, -elt, -ild, -old, -aw, -awn, -ew, -ow, -own		
Lesson 30: Which Word Does Not Rhyme?		
Lesson 31: Rhyming and Word Families Picture Match		
Lesson 32: Rhyming and Word Families Final Review		

Rhyming and Word Families Mini-Assessments Recording Sheets (p. 1)

Student Name: _____ Grade: ____ Teacher: _____

Use these sheets to document the student's progression through the intervention.

Lesson 1: Hearing Three Letter Words that Rhyme -at, -ad, -ag

Assessment: Use the following chart to assess this activity. Place a '√' next to each word-ending every time the student is able to identify two words from that family that rhyme. The student has mastered this lesson if he/she can accurately identify pairs of rhyming words consistently without assistance at least 5 consecutive times.

-at							-ad							-ag					

Date Mastered: _____

Lesson 2: Hearing Three Letter Words that Rhyme -ed, -en, -et

Assessment: Use the following chart to assess this activity. Place a '√' next to each word-ending every time the student is able to identify two words from that family that rhyme. The student has mastered this lesson if he/she can accurately identify pairs of rhyming words consistently without assistance at least 5 consecutive times.

-ed							-en							-et					

Date Mastered: _____

Lesson 3: Hearing Three Letter Words that Rhyme -ig, -id, -ib

Assessment: Use the following chart to assess this activity. Place a '√' next to each word-ending every time the student is able to identify two words from that family that rhyme. The student has mastered this lesson if he/she can accurately identify pairs of rhyming words consistently without assistance at least 5 consecutive times.

-ig							-id							-ib					

Date Mastered: _____

Lesson 4: Hearing Three Letter Words that Rhyme -og, -ot, -od

Assessment: Use the following chart to assess this activity. Place a '√' next to each word-ending every time the student is able to identify two words from that family that rhyme. The student has mastered this lesson if he/she can accurately identify pairs of rhyming words consistently without assistance at least 5 consecutive times.

-og							-ot							-od					

Date Mastered: _____

Lesson 5: Hearing Three Letter Words that Rhyme -ub, -ug, -um

Assessment: Use the following chart to assess this activity. Place a '√' next to each word-ending every time the student is able to identify two words from that family that rhyme. The student has mastered this lesson if he/she can accurately identify pairs of rhyming words consistently without assistance at least 5 consecutive times.

-ub							-ug							-um					

Date Mastered: _____

Lesson 6: **Saying** Words that Rhyme -at, -ad, -ag, -ed, -en, -et, -ig, -id, -ib, -og, -ot, -od, -ub, -ug, -um

Assessment: Use the following chart to assess this activity. Place a '√' next to each word-end each time the student is able to say two words from that family that rhyme. The student has mastered this lesson if he/she can accurately say pairs of rhyming words consistently without assistance at least 3 consecutive times. **THIS LESSON IS EXTREMELY IMPORTANT. BE SURE THE STUDENT CAN AUTOMATICALLY HEAR AND SAY PAIRS OF RHYMING WORDS BEFORE MOVING ON TO THE NEXT LESSON.**

-at				-et				-ot			
-ad				-ig				-od			
-ag				-id				-ub			
-ed				-ib				-ug			
-en				-og				-um			

Date Mastered: _____

Lesson 7: Hearing More Words that Rhyme -all, -alm, -ill, -old, -oll, -ell, -elp, -ull

Assessment: Use the following chart to assess this activity. Place a '√' next to each word-ending every time the student is able to identify two words from that family that rhyme. The student has mastered this lesson if he/she can accurately identify pairs of rhyming words consistently without assistance at least 5 consecutive times.

-all					-alm					-ill				
-old					-oll					-ell				
-elp					-ull									

Date Mastered: _____

Rhyming and Word Families Mini-Assessments Recording Sheets (p. 2)

Student Name: _____

Lesson 8: Hearing More Words that Rhyme -and, -ang, -ank, -ing, -ink, -int

Assessment: Use the following chart to assess this activity. Place a '√' next to each word-ending every time the student is able to identify two words from that family that rhyme. The student has mastered this lesson if he/she can accurately identify pairs of rhyming words consistently without assistance at least 5 consecutive times.

-and					
-ing					

-ang					
-ink					

-ank					
-int					

Date Mastered: _____

Lesson 9: Hearing More Words that Rhyme -ond, -ong, -end, -ung, -unk, -ant

Assessment: Use the following chart to assess this activity. Place a '√' next to each word-ending every time the student is able to identify two words from that family that rhyme. The student has mastered this lesson if he/she can accurately identify pairs of rhyming words consistently without assistance at least 5 consecutive times.

-ond					
-ong					

-end					
-ung					

-unk					
-ant					

Date Mastered: _____

Lesson 10: Hearing More Words that Rhyme -art, -ast, -ift, -irt, -ist, -ort

Assessment: Use the following chart to assess this activity. Place a '√' next to each word-ending every time the student is able to identify two words from that family that rhyme. The student has mastered this lesson if he/she can accurately identify pairs of rhyming words consistently without assistance at least 5 consecutive times.

-art					
-ast					

-ift					
-irt					

-ist					
-ort					

Date Mastered: _____

Lesson 11: Hearing More Words that Rhyme -ost, -eft, -elt, -est, -ust, -ass

Assessment: Use the following chart to assess this activity. Place a '√' next to each word-ending every time the student is able to identify two words from that family that rhyme. The student has mastered this lesson if he/she can accurately identify pairs of rhyming words consistently without assistance at least 5 consecutive times.

-ost					
-eft					

-elt					
-est					

-ust					
-ass					

Date Mastered: _____

Lesson 12: Hearing More Words that Rhyme -amp, -iss, -oss, -omp, -ess, -ump

Assessment: Use the following chart to assess this activity. Place a '√' next to each word-ending every time the student is able to identify two words from that family that rhyme. The student has mastered this lesson if he/she can accurately identify pairs of rhyming words consistently without assistance at least 5 consecutive times.

-amp					
-iss					

-oss					
-omp					

-ess					
-ump					

Date Mastered: _____

Lesson 13: Saying More Words that Rhyme -all, -alm, -ill, -old, -oll, -ell, -elp, -ull, -and, -ang, -ank, -ing, -ink, -int, -ond, -ong, -end, -ung, -unk, -ant, -art, -ast, -ift, -irt, -ist, -ort, -ost, -eft, -elt, -est, -ust, -ass, -amp, -iss, -oss, -omp, -ess, -ump,

Assessment: Use the following chart to assess this activity. Place a '√' next to each word-ending every time the student is able to say two words from that family that rhyme. The student has mastered this lesson if he/she can accurately say pairs of rhyming words consistently without assistance at least 2 consecutive times. **THIS LESSON IS EXTREMELY IMPORTANT. BE SURE THE STUDENT CAN AUTOMATICALLY HEAR AND SAY PAIRS OF RHYMING WORDS BEFORE MOVING ON TO THE NEXT LESSON.**

-all			-and			-end			-ist			-end			-amp		
-alm			-ang			-ung			-ort			-ung			-iss		
-ill			-ank			-unk			-ost			-unk			-oss		
-old			-ing			-ant			-eft			-ant			-omp		
-oll			-ink			-art			-elt			-art			-ess		
-ell			-int			-ast			-est			-ast			-ump		
-elp			-ond			-ift			-ust			-ift					
-ull			-ong			-irt			-ass			-irt					

Date Mastered: _____

Student Name: _____

Lesson 14: Hearing Even More Words that Rhyme *-ash, -ath, -atch, -arch, -ish, -ith*

Assessment: Use the following chart to assess this activity. Place a '√' next to each word-ending every time the student is able to identify two words from that family that rhyme. The student has mastered this lesson if he/she can accurately identify pairs of rhyming words consistently without assistance at least 5 consecutive times.

-ash							-arch					
-ath							-ish					
-atch							-ith					

Date Mastered: _____

Lesson 15: Hearing Even More Words that Rhyme *-itch, -irth, -osh, -otch, -oth, -orch*

Assessment: Use the following chart to assess this activity. Place a '√' next to each word-ending every time the student is able to identify two words from that family that rhyme. The student has mastered this lesson if he/she can accurately identify pairs of rhyming words consistently without assistance at least 5 consecutive times.

-itch							-otch					
-irth							-oth					
-osh							-orch					

Date Mastered: _____

Lesson 16: Hearing Long Vowel Rhyming Words *-ace, -ade, -age, -ake, -ale, -ame, -ape*

Assessment: Use the following chart to assess this activity. Place a '√' next to each word-ending every time the student is able to identify two words from that family that rhyme. The student has mastered this lesson if he/she can accurately identify pairs of rhyming words consistently without assistance at least 5 consecutive times.

-ace							-ale					
-ade							-ame					
-age							-ape					
-ake												

Date Mastered: _____

Lesson 17: Hearing Long Vowel Rhyming Words *-ate, -ice, -ide, -ife, -ile, -ine, -ite*

Assessment: Use the following chart to assess this activity. Place a '√' next to each word-ending every time the student is able to identify two words from that family that rhyme. The student has mastered this lesson if he/she can accurately identify pairs of rhyming words consistently without assistance at least 5 consecutive times.

-ate							-ile					
-ice							-ine					
-ide							-ite					
-ife												

Date Mastered: _____

Lesson 18: Hearing Long Vowel Rhyming Words *-ive, -ode, -oke, -ole, -one, -ope, -ote*

Assessment: Use the following chart to assess this activity. Place a '√' next to each word-ending every time the student is able to identify two words from that family that rhyme. The student has mastered this lesson if he/she can accurately identify pairs of rhyming words consistently without assistance at least 5 consecutive times.

-ive							-one					
-ode							-ope					
-oke							-ote					
-ole												

Date Mastered: _____

Lesson 19: Hearing <u>Special</u> Long Vowel Rhyming Words *-aid, -ail, -ain, -ait, -ay, -eat, -each*

Assessment: Use the following chart to assess this activity. Place a '√' next to each word-ending every time the student is able to identify two words from that family that rhyme. The student has mastered this lesson if he/she can accurately identify pairs of rhyming words consistently without assistance at least 5 consecutive times.

-aid							-ay					
-ail							-eat					
-ain							-each					
-ait												

Date Mastered: _____

Rhyming and Word Families Mini-Assessments Recording Sheets (p. 4)

Student Name: _____

Lesson 20: Hearing <u>Special</u> Long Vowel Rhyming Words -ead, -eak, -eam, -ean, -eet, -eed, -eek

Assessment: Use the following chart to assess this activity. Place a '√' next to each word-ending every time the student is able to identify two words from that family that rhyme. The student has mastered this lesson if he/she can accurately identify pairs of rhyming words consistently without assistance at least 5 consecutive times.

-ead					
-eak					
-eam					
-ean					

-eet					
-eed					
-eek					

Date Mastered: _____

Lesson 21: Hearing <u>Special</u> Long Vowel Rhyming Words -eel, -eem, -eep, -oach, -oad, -oam, -oan, oat

Assessment: Use the following chart to assess this activity. Place a '√' next to each word-ending every time the student is able to identify two words from that family that rhyme. The student has mastered this lesson if he/she can accurately identify pairs of rhyming words consistently without assistance at least 5 consecutive times.

-eel					
-eem					
-eep					
-oach					

-oad					
-oam					
-oan					
-oat					

Date Mastered: _____

Lesson 22: Saying Even More Words that Rhyme -ash, -ath, -atch, -arch, -ish, -ith, -itch, -irth, -osh, -otch, -oth, -orch, -ace, -ade, -age, -ake, -ale, -ame, -ape, -ate, -ice, -ide, -ife, -ile, -ine, -ite, -ive, -ode, -oke, -ole, -one, -ope, -ote, -aid, -ail, -ain, -ait, -ay, -eat, -each, -ead, -eak, -eam, -ean, -eet, -eed, -eek, -eel, -eem, -eep, -oach, -oad, -oam, -oan, -oat

Assessment: Use the following chart to assess this activity. Place a '√' next to each word-ending every time the student is able to say two words from that family that rhyme. The student has mastered this lesson if he/she can accurately say pairs of rhyming words consistently without assistance at least 2 consecutive times. THIS LESSON IS EXTREMELY IMPORTANT. BE SURE THE STUDENT CAN AUTOMATICALLY HEAR AND SAY PAIRS OF RHYMING WORDS BEFORE MOVING ON TO THE NEXT LESSON.

-ash			-oth			-ate			-oke			-ay			-eek		
-ath			-orch			-ice			-ole			-eat			-eel		
-atch			-ace			-ide			-one			-each			-eem		
-arch			-ade			-ife			-ope			-ead			-eep		
-ish			-age			-ile			-ote			-eak			-oach		
-ith			-ake			-ine			-aid			-eam			-oad		
-itch			-ale			-ite			-ail			-ean			-oam		
-irth			-ame			-ive			-ain			-eet			-oan		
-osh			-ape			-ode			-ait			-eed			-oat		

Date Mastered: _____

Lesson 23: Hearing Special Rhyming Words -oil, -oin, -oint, -oist, -oot, -ook, -oom

Assessment: Use the following chart to assess this activity. Place a '√' next to each word-ending every time the student is able to identify two words from that family that rhyme. The student has mastered this lesson if he/she can accurately identify pairs of rhyming words consistently without assistance at least 5 consecutive times.

-oil					
-oin					
-oint					
-oist					

-oot					
-ook					
-oom					

Date Mastered: _____

Lesson 24: Hearing Special Rhyming Words -ound, -our, -ouse, -out, -oon, -oop

Assessment: Use the following chart to assess this activity. Place a '√' next to each word-ending every time the student is able to identify two words from that family that rhyme. The student has mastered this lesson if he/she can accurately identify pairs of rhyming words consistently without assistance at least 5 consecutive times.

-ound				
-our				

-ouse				
-out				

-oon				
-oop				

Date Mastered: _____

Student Name: _____

Lesson 25: Hearing Special r-Controlled Rhyming Words *-ar, -ard, -arm, -arn, -art, -er, -ern*

Assessment: Use the following chart to assess this activity. Place a '√' next to each word-ending every time the student is able to identify two words from that family that rhyme. The student has mastered this lesson if he/she can accurately identify pairs of rhyming words consistently without assistance at least 5 consecutive times.

-ar							-art					
-ard							-er					
-arm							-ern					
-arn												

Date Mastered: _____

Lesson 26: Hearing Special r-Controlled Rhyming Words *-ird, -irt, -or, -ord, -ork, -orn, -ir, -ur*

Assessment: Use the following chart to assess this activity. Place a '√' next to each word-ending every time the student is able to identify two words from that family that rhyme. The student has mastered this lesson if he/she can accurately identify pairs of rhyming words consistently without assistance at least 5 consecutive times.

-ird							-ork					
-irt							-orn					
-or							-ir					
-ord							-ur					

Date Mastered: _____

Lesson 27: Hearing Special l-Controlled Rhyming Words *-ald, -alk, -eld, -elt, -ild, -old*

Assessment: Use the following chart to assess this activity. Place a '√' next to each word-ending every time the student is able to identify two words from that family that rhyme. The student has mastered this lesson if he/she can accurately identify pairs of rhyming words consistently without assistance at least 5 consecutive times.

-ald							-elt					
-alk							-ild					
-eld							-old					

Date Mastered: _____

Lesson 28: Hearing Special w-Controlled Rhyming Words *-aw, -awn, -ew, -ow, -own*

Assessment: Use the following chart to assess this activity. Place a '√' next to each word-ending every time the student is able to identify two words from that family that rhyme. The student has mastered this lesson if he/she can accurately identify pairs of rhyming words consistently without assistance at least 5 consecutive times.

-aw							-ow				
-awn							-own				
-ew											

Date Mastered: _____

Lesson 29: Saying Even More Words that Rhyme *-oil, -oin, -oint, -oist, -oot, -ook, -oom, -ound, -our, -ouse, -out, -oon, -oop, -ar, -ard, -arm, -arn, -art, -er, -ern, -ird, -irt, -or, -ord, -ork, -orn, -ir, -ur, -ald, -alk, -eld, -elt, -ild, -old, -aw, -awn, -ew, -ow, -own*

Assessment: Use the following chart to assess this activity. Place a '√' next to each word-ending every time the student is able to say two words from that family that rhyme. The student has mastered this lesson if he/she can accurately say pairs of rhyming words consistently without assistance at least 2 consecutive times. **THIS LESSON IS EXTREMELY IMPORTANT. BE SURE THE STUDENT CAN AUTOMATICALLY HEAR AND SAY PAIRS OF RHYMING WORDS BEFORE MOVING ON TO THE NEXT LESSON.**

-oil			-ound			-ard			-irt			-ald			-awn		
-oin			-our			-arm			-or			-alk			-ew		
-oint			-ouse			-arn			-ord			-eld			-ow		
-oist			-out			-art			-ork			-elt			-own		
-oot			-oon			-er			-orn			-ild			Date		
-ook			-oop			-ern			-ir			-old			Mastered:		
-oom			-ar			-ird			-ur			-aw			_____		

Student Name: _____

Lesson 30: Which Word Does Not Rhyme?

Assessment: Use the following chart to assess this activity. Say each group of words and circle the word that does not rhyme with the other two when the student accurately identifies it. The student has mastered this lesson if he/she can accurately identify the non-rhyming word in a set of three words.

mouse/house/home	toy/van/boy	wet/hat/pat	pig/hog/log	hug/goat/boat
vase/hate/trace	round/tall/ball	bid/feed/lid	eat/seek/beak	bond/pond/frog
horse/dirt/hurt	play/day/sun	limb/leaf/grief	found/word/bound	book/hook/jerk
grin/fly/sly	truck/ice/slice	mold/cold/ice	meat/glide/slide	led/good/fed

Date Mastered: _____

Lesson 31: Rhyming and Word Families Picture Match

Assessment: Use the chart below to assess this activity. Have the student use the rhyming picture sheet on page 60. Begin by having him/her say the name of each picture in the first row. Have him/her identify the pictures that rhyme with the first picture in the row (there may be more than one that rhymes). Place a '√' under the pictures the student gets correct (on the chart below). Continue in like manner for rows 2, 3, and 4. The student has mastered this lesson if he/she can accurately identify and say the pictures/words that rhyme with the first picture of each row.

rose	broom	nose	price
cat	rice	bat	hat
phone	bone	duck	pants
bed	sleep	globe	sled

Date Mastered: _____

Lesson 32: Rhyming and Word Families Final Review

This lesson is assessed through the use of picture cards, picture books, or magazine/newspaper pictures. The student has mastered this lesson if he/she can easily and accurately identify words that rhyme using pictures **and** if he/she can orally say them. HAVE FUN FINDING PAIRS OF RHYMING WORDS!

Date Mastered: _____

Rhyming and Word Families Intervention Lessons

Use the following 32 lessons to guide you through the rhyming and word families intervention. Remember, the intervention is individualized to the student's needs and must be implemented at the student's pace. Don't move to a new lesson until mastery of the current lesson is achieved. Teaching to MASTERY is the goal.

To determine whether or not mastery of each lesson has been achieved, use the 'Rhyming and Word Families Mini-Assessments Recording Sheets' (pages 21-26) to measure the student's proficiency before beginning a new lesson.

Rhyming and Word Families: Lesson 1

Lesson Name: Hearing Three Letter Words that Rhyme -at, -ad, -ag

Description of Lesson/Activity: Through repeated exposure to rhyming words, the student identifies words that are from the same word family.

Procedures for Implementing the Activity:

STEP ONE: Briefly review with student basic letter recognition and letter sounds skills. Have the student state the **name and sounds** of letters or blends as you point to them using a letter or blends chart. Explain to student that letters go together to form words and that many words belong to families. Explain that words who come from the same family all sound alike because their ending sounds match. Explain that today he/she will learn words from three different word families.

STEP TWO: Show the student the letters 'at' (using magnetic letters, foam letters, letter cards, paper-pencil, etc.). Have student say the sounds for both letters using a short ă sound. Say the two letters blended together and have the student repeat. Tell the student that there are many words that end with the 'at' sound. Say several 'at' family words and point to the letters on display in front of the student as each word is pronounced.

STEP THREE: On a piece of paper write the word **YES** on the left side and **NO** on the right. Say several three-letter words. Have the student point to the word **YES** if the word is part of the targeted word family and **NO** if it is not. Have student repeat each word that is part of the word family. Continue saying one-syllable words until the student can confidently identify the words that are part of the targeted word family without hesitation.

STEP FOUR: Explain to student that words that are part of the same word family are called **rhyming** words. Say two words (one of which is a member of the targeted word family) and have the student say whether or not they rhyme. Continue saying pairs of words and have the student say YES if they rhyme and NO if they don't rhyme.

STEP FIVE: Repeat steps two, three, and four with the word families -ad and -ag

STEP SIX: Assess the student to ascertain whether or not mastery of this lesson has been achieved. Follow the assessment directions and record the results on the 'Rhyming and Word Families Mini-Assessments Recording Sheet'. If the student has mastered this lesson, move on to the next lesson. If the student has NOT mastered this lesson, repeat lesson until mastery has been obtained.

TEACHING TO MASTERY IS THE GOAL

Rhyming and Word Families: Lesson 2

Lesson Name: Hearing Three Letter Words that Rhyme *-ed, -en, -et*

Description of Lesson/Activity: Through repeated exposure to rhyming words, the student identifies words that are from the same word family.

Procedures for Implementing the Activity:

STEP ONE: <u>Briefly</u> review with student basic letter recognition and letter sounds skills. Have the student state the **name and sounds** of letters or blends as you point to them using a letter or blends chart. Explain to student that letters go together to form words and that many words belong to families. Explain that words who come from the same family all sound alike because their ending sounds match. Explain that today he/she will learn words from three different word families.

STEP TWO: Show the student the letters 'ed' (using magnetic letters, foam letters, letter cards, paper-pencil, etc.). Have student say the sounds for both letters using a short ĕ sound. Say the two letters blended together and have the student repeat. Tell the student that there are many words that end with the 'ed' sound. Say several 'ed' family words and point to the letters on display in front of the student as each word is pronounced.

STEP THREE: On a piece of paper write the word **YES** on the left side and **NO** on the right. Say several three-letter words. Have the student point to the word **YES** if the word is part of the targeted word family and **NO** if it is not. Have student repeat each word that is part of the word family. Continue saying one-syllable words until the student can confidently identify the words that are part of the targeted word family without hesitation.

STEP FOUR: Explain to student that words that are part of the same word family are called **rhyming** words. Say two words (one of which is a member of the targeted word family) and have the student say whether or not they rhyme. Continue saying pairs of words and have the student say YES if they rhyme and NO if they don't rhyme.

STEP FIVE: Repeat steps two, three, and four with the word families *-en* and *-et*

STEP SIX: Assess the student to ascertain whether or not mastery of this lesson has been achieved. Follow the assessment directions and record the results on the 'Rhyming and Word Families Mini-Assessments Recording Sheet'. If the student has mastered this lesson, move on to the next lesson. If the student has NOT mastered this lesson, repeat lesson until mastery has been obtained.

<u>TEACHING TO MASTERY IS THE GOAL</u>

Rhyming and Word Families: Lesson 3

Lesson Name: Hearing Three Letter Words that Rhyme *-ig, -id, -ib*

Description of Lesson/Activity: Through repeated exposure to rhyming words, the student identifies words that are from the same word family.

Procedures for Implementing the Activity:

STEP ONE: Briefly review with student basic letter recognition and letter sounds skills. Have the student state the **name and sounds** of letters or blends as you point to them using a letter or blends chart. Explain to student that letters go together to form words and that many words belong to families. Explain that words who come from the same family all sound alike because their ending sounds match. Explain that today he/she will learn words from three different word families.

STEP TWO: Show the student the letters 'ig' (using magnetic letters, foam letters, letter cards, paper-pencil, etc.). Have student say the sounds for both letters using a short ĭ sound. Say the two letters blended together and have the student repeat. Tell the student that there are many words that end with the 'ig' sound. Say several 'ig' family words and point to the letters on display in front of the student as each word is pronounced.

STEP THREE: On a piece of paper write the word **YES** on the left side and **NO** on the right. Say several three-letter words. Have the student point to the word **YES** if the word is part of the targeted word family and **NO** if it is not. Have student repeat each word that is part of the word family. Continue saying one-syllable words until the student can confidently identify the words that are part of the targeted word family without hesitation.

STEP FOUR: Explain to student that words that are part of the same word family are called **rhyming** words. Say two words (one of which is a member of the targeted word family) and have the student say whether or not they rhyme. Continue saying pairs of words and have the student say YES if they rhyme and NO if they don't rhyme.

STEP FIVE: Repeat steps two, three, and four with the word families *-id* and *-ib*

STEP SIX: Assess the student to ascertain whether or not mastery of this lesson has been achieved. Follow the assessment directions and record the results on the 'Rhyming and Word Families Mini-Assessments Recording Sheet'. If the student has mastered this lesson, move on to the next lesson. If the student has NOT mastered this lesson, repeat lesson until mastery has been obtained.

TEACHING TO MASTERY IS THE GOAL

Rhyming and Word Families: Lesson 4

Lesson Name: Hearing Three Letter Words that Rhyme -og, -ot, -od

Description of Lesson/Activity: Through repeated exposure to rhyming words, the student identifies words that are from the same word family.

Procedures for Implementing the Activity:
STEP ONE: Briefly review with student basic letter recognition and letter sounds skills. Have the student state the **name and sounds** of letters or blends as you point to them using a letter or blends chart. Explain to student that letters go together to form words and that many words belong to families. Explain that words who come from the same family all sound alike because their ending sounds match. Explain that today he/she will learn words from three different word families.

STEP TWO: Show the student the letters 'og' (using magnetic letters, foam letters, letter cards, paper-pencil, etc.). Have student say the sounds for both letters using a short ŏ sound. Say the two letters blended together and have the student repeat. Tell the student that there are many words that end with the 'og' sound. Say several 'og' family words and point to the letters on display in front of the student as each word is pronounced.

STEP THREE: On a piece of paper write the word **YES** on the left side and **NO** on the right. Say several three-letter words. Have the student point to the word **YES** if the word is part of the targeted word family and **NO** if it is not. Have student repeat each word that is part of the word family. Continue saying one-syllable words until the student can confidently identify the words that are part of the targeted word family without hesitation.

STEP FOUR: Explain to student that words that are part of the same word family are called **rhyming** words. Say two words (one of which is a member of the targeted word family) and have the student say whether or not they rhyme. Continue saying pairs of words and have the student say YES if they rhyme and NO if they don't rhyme.

STEP FIVE: Repeat steps two, three, and four with the word families -ot and -od

STEP SIX: Assess the student to ascertain whether or not mastery of this lesson has been achieved. Follow the assessment directions and record the results on the 'Rhyming and Word Families Mini-Assessments Recording Sheet'. If the student has mastered this lesson, move on to the next lesson. If the student has NOT mastered this lesson, repeat lesson until mastery has been obtained.

TEACHING TO MASTERY IS THE GOAL

Rhyming and Word Families: Lesson 5

Lesson Name: Hearing Three Letter Words that Rhyme *-ub, -ug, -um*

Description of Lesson/Activity: Through repeated exposure to rhyming words, the student identifies words that are from the same word family.

Procedures for Implementing the Activity:
STEP ONE: <u>Briefly</u> review with student basic letter recognition and letter sounds skills. Have the student state the **name and sounds** of letters or blends as you point to them using a letter or blends chart. Explain to student that letters go together to form words and that many words belong to families. Explain that words who come from the same family all sound alike because their ending sounds match. Explain that today he/she will learn words from three different word families.

STEP TWO: Show the student the letters 'ub' (using magnetic letters, foam letters, letter cards, paper-pencil, etc.). Have student say the sounds for both letters using a short ŭ sound. Say the two letters blended together and have the student repeat. Tell the student that there are many words that end with the 'ub' sound. Say several 'ub' family words and point to the letters on display in front of the student as each word is pronounced.

STEP THREE: On a piece of paper write the word **YES** on the left side and **NO** on the right. Say several three-letter words. Have the student point to the word **YES** if the word is part of the targeted word family and **NO** if it is not. Have student repeat each word that is part of the word family. Continue saying one-syllable words until the student can confidently identify the words that are part of the targeted word family without hesitation.

STEP FOUR: Explain to student that words that are part of the same word family are called **rhyming** words. Say two words (one of which is a member of the targeted word family) and have the student say whether or not they rhyme. Continue saying pairs of words and have the student say YES if they rhyme and NO if they don't rhyme.

STEP FIVE: Repeat steps two, three, and four with the word families *-ug* and *-um*

STEP SIX: Assess the student to ascertain whether or not mastery of this lesson has been achieved. Follow the assessment directions and record the results on the 'Rhyming and Word Families Mini-Assessments Recording Sheet'. If the student has mastered this lesson, move on to the next lesson. If the student has NOT mastered this lesson, repeat lesson until mastery has been obtained.

<u>TEACHING TO MASTERY IS THE GOAL</u>

Rhyming and Word Families: Lesson 6

Lesson Name: **Saying** Words that Rhyme *-at, -ad, -ag, -ed, -en, -et, -ig, -id, -ib, -og, -ot, -od, -ub, -ug, -um*

Description of Lesson/Activity: Through repeated exposure to word family words, the student orally states pairs of words that rhyme.

Procedures for Implementing the Activity:

STEP ONE: Explain to student that today he/she will practice saying rhyming words. Tell the student that he/she will say words from the word families learned in lessons 1-5.

STEP TWO: On a piece of paper (or using letter cards, tiles, etc.) write one of the word endings focused on in lessons 1-5. Pronounce the word family and have the student repeat.

STEP THREE: Model for the student how you can say two words from that word family that rhyme. First, say the word ending. Next say one word from that family. Then say another word from that family. Finally restate the word ending. (Example: "at" ... "cat" ... "bat" ... "at")

STEP FOUR: Explain to student that he/she will do the same with other word families. Assist the student when he/she has trouble thinking of words that rhyme. Spend AMPLE time on this step to ensure the student has a firm grasp on the concept of rhyming. **DRILL AND PRACTICE!! DRILL AND PRACTICE!! DRILL AND PRACTICE!!**

STEP FIVE: Assess the student to ascertain whether or not mastery of this lesson has been achieved. Follow the assessment directions and record the results on the 'Rhyming and Word Families Mini-Assessments Recording Sheet'. If the student has mastered this lesson, move on to the next lesson. If the student has NOT mastered this lesson, repeat lesson until mastery has been obtained.

<u>TEACHING TO MASTERY IS THE GOAL</u>

Rhyming and Word Families: Lesson 7

Lesson Name: Hearing More Words that Rhyme -all, -alm, -ill, -old, -oll, -ell, -elp, -ull

Description of Lesson/Activity: Through repeated exposure to rhyming words, the student identifies words that are from the same word family.

Procedures for Implementing the Activity:
STEP ONE: Briefly review with student basic letter recognition and letter sounds skills. Have the student state the **name and sounds** of letters or blends as you point to them using a letter or blends chart. Explain to student that letters go together to form words and that many words belong to families. Explain that words who come from the same family all sound alike because their ending sounds match. Explain that today he/she will learn words from eight different word families.

STEP TWO: Show the student the letters 'all' (using magnetic letters, foam letters, letter cards, paper-pencil, etc.). Have student say the sounds for all of the letters. Say the letters blended together and have the student repeat. Tell the student that there are many words that end with the 'all' sound. Say several 'all' family words by putting both single consonants and consonant blends in front of the sound. Point to the letters on display in front of the student as each word is pronounced.

STEP THREE: On a piece of paper write the word **YES** on the left side and **NO** on the right. Say several one syllable words. Have the student point to the word **YES** if the word is part of the targeted word family and **NO** if it is not. Have student repeat each word that is part of the word family. Continue saying one-syllable words until the student can confidently identify the words that are part of the targeted word family without hesitation.

STEP FOUR: Explain to student that words that are part of the same word family are called **rhyming** words. Say two words (one of which is a member of the targeted word family) and have the student say whether or not they rhyme. Continue saying pairs of words and have the student say YES if they rhyme and NO if they don't rhyme.

STEP FIVE: Repeat steps two, three, and four with the word families -alm, -ill, -old, -oll, -ell, -elp, and -ull

STEP SIX: Assess the student to ascertain whether or not mastery of this lesson has been achieved. Follow the assessment directions and record the results on the 'Rhyming and Word Families Mini-Assessments Recording Sheet'. If the student has mastered this lesson, move on to the next lesson. If the student has NOT mastered this lesson, repeat lesson until mastery has been obtained.

<u>TEACHING TO MASTERY IS THE GOAL</u>

Rhyming and Word Families: Lesson 8

Lesson Name: Hearing More Words that Rhyme -and, -ang, -ank, -ing, -ink, -int

Description of Lesson/Activity: Through repeated exposure to rhyming words, the student identifies words that are from the same word family.

Procedures for Implementing the Activity:

STEP ONE: <u>Briefly</u> review with student basic letter recognition and letter sounds skills. Have the student state the **name and sounds** of letters or blends as you point to them using a letter or blends chart. Explain to student that letters go together to form words and that many words belong to families. Explain that words who come from the same family all sound alike because their ending sounds match. Explain that today he/she will learn words from six different word families.

STEP TWO: Show the student the letters 'and' (using magnetic letters, foam letters, letter cards, paper-pencil, etc.). Have student say the sounds for all of the letters. Say the letters blended together and have the student repeat. Tell the student that there are many words that end with the 'and' sound. Say several 'and' family words by putting both single consonants and consonant blends in front of the sound. Point to the letters on display in front of the student as each word is pronounced.

STEP THREE: On a piece of paper write the word **YES** on the left side and **NO** on the right. Say several one syllable words. Have the student point to the word **YES** if the word is part of the targeted word family and **NO** if it is not. Have student repeat each word that is part of the word family. Continue saying one-syllable words until the student can confidently identify the words that are part of the targeted word family without hesitation.

STEP FOUR: Explain to student that words that are part of the same word family are called **rhyming** words. Say two words (one of which is a member of the targeted word family) and have the student say whether or not they rhyme. Continue saying pairs of words and have the student say YES if they rhyme and NO if they don't rhyme.

STEP FIVE: Repeat steps two, three, and four with the word families -and, -ang, -ank, -ing, -ink, and -int.

STEP SIX: Assess the student to ascertain whether or not mastery of this lesson has been achieved. Follow the assessment directions and record the results on the 'Rhyming and Word Families Mini-Assessments Recording Sheet'. If the student has mastered this lesson, move on to the next lesson. If the student has NOT mastered this lesson, repeat lesson until mastery has been obtained.

<u>TEACHING TO MASTERY IS THE GOAL</u>

Rhyming and Word Families: Lesson 9

Lesson Name: Hearing More Words that Rhyme -ond, -ong, -end, -ung, -unk, -ant

Description of Lesson/Activity: Through repeated exposure to rhyming words, the student identifies words that are from the same word family.

Procedures for Implementing the Activity:

STEP ONE: <u>Briefly</u> review with student basic letter recognition and letter sounds skills. Have the student state the **name and sounds** of letters or blends as you point to them using a letter or blends chart. Explain to student that letters go together to form words and that many words belong to families. Explain that words who come from the same family all sound alike because their ending sounds match. Explain that today he/she will learn words from six different word families.

STEP TWO: Show the student the letters 'ond' (using magnetic letters, foam letters, letter cards, paper-pencil, etc.). Have student say the sounds for all of the letters. Say the letters blended together and have the student repeat. Tell the student that there are many words that end with the 'ond' sound. Say several 'ond' family words by putting both single consonants and consonant blends in front of the sound. Point to the letters on display in front of the student as each word is pronounced.

STEP THREE: On a piece of paper write the word **YES** on the left side and **NO** on the right. Say several one syllable words. Have the student point to the word **YES** if the word is part of the targeted word family and **NO** if it is not. Have student repeat each word that is part of the word family. Continue saying one-syllable words until the student can confidently identify the words that are part of the targeted word family without hesitation.

STEP FOUR: Explain to student that words that are part of the same word family are called **rhyming** words. Say two words (one of which is a member of the targeted word family) and have the student say whether or not they rhyme. Continue saying pairs of words and have the student say YES if they rhyme and NO if they don't rhyme.

STEP FIVE: Repeat steps two, three, and four with the word families *-ong, -end, -ung, -unk,* and *-ant.*

STEP SIX: Assess the student to ascertain whether or not mastery of this lesson has been achieved. Follow the assessment directions and record the results on the 'Rhyming and Word Families Mini-Assessments Recording Sheet'. If the student has mastered this lesson, move on to the next lesson. If the student has NOT mastered this lesson, repeat lesson until mastery has been obtained.

<u>TEACHING TO MASTERY IS THE GOAL</u>

Rhyming and Word Families: Lesson 10

Lesson Name: Hearing More Words that Rhyme *-art, -ast, -ift, -irt, -ist, -ort*

Description of Lesson/Activity: Through repeated exposure to rhyming words, the student identifies words that are from the same word family.

Procedures for Implementing the Activity:

STEP ONE: <u>Briefly</u> review with student basic letter recognition and letter sounds skills. Have the student state the **name and sounds** of letters or blends as you point to them using a letter or blends chart. Explain to student that letters go together to form words and that many words belong to families. Explain that words who come from the same family all sound alike because their ending sounds match. Explain that today he/she will learn words from six different word families.

STEP TWO: Show the student the letters 'art' (using magnetic letters, foam letters, letter cards, paper-pencil, etc.). Have student say the sounds for all of the letters. Say the letters blended together and have the student repeat. Tell the student that there are many words that end with the 'art' sound. Say several 'art' family words by putting both single consonants and consonant blends in front of the sound. Point to the letters on display in front of the student as each word is pronounced.

STEP THREE: On a piece of paper write the word **YES** on the left side and **NO** on the right. Say several one syllable words. Have the student point to the word **YES** if the word is part of the targeted word family and **NO** if it is not. Have student repeat each word that is part of the word family. Continue saying one-syllable words until the student can confidently identify the words that are part of the targeted word family without hesitation.

STEP FOUR: Explain to student that words that are part of the same word family are called **rhyming** words. Say two words (one of which is a member of the targeted word family) and have the student say whether or not they rhyme. Continue saying pairs of words and have the student say YES if they rhyme and NO if they don't rhyme.

STEP FIVE: Repeat steps two, three, and four with the word families , *-ast, -ift, -irt, -ist,* and *-ort.*

STEP SIX: Assess the student to ascertain whether or not mastery of this lesson has been achieved. Follow the assessment directions and record the results on the 'Rhyming and Word Families Mini-Assessments Recording Sheet'. If the student has mastered this lesson, move on to the next lesson. If the student has NOT mastered this lesson, repeat lesson until mastery has been obtained.

<u>TEACHING TO MASTERY IS THE GOAL</u>

Rhyming and Word Families: Lesson 11

Lesson Name: Hearing More Words that Rhyme *-ost, -eft, -elt, -est, -ust, -ass*

Description of Lesson/Activity: Through repeated exposure to rhyming words, the student identifies words that are from the same word family.

Procedures for Implementing the Activity:

STEP ONE: <u>Briefly</u> review with student basic letter recognition and letter sounds skills. Have the student state the **name and sounds** of letters or blends as you point to them using a letter or blends chart. Explain to student that letters go together to form words and that many words belong to families. Explain that words who come from the same family all sound alike because their ending sounds match. Explain that today he/she will learn words from six different word families.

STEP TWO: Show the student the letters 'ost' (using magnetic letters, foam letters, letter cards, paper-pencil, etc.). Have student say the sounds for all of the letters. Say the letters blended together and have the student repeat. Tell the student that there are many words that end with the 'ost' sound. Say several 'ost' family words by putting both single consonants and consonant blends in front of the sound. Point to the letters on display in front of the student as each word is pronounced.

STEP THREE: On a piece of paper write the word **YES** on the left side and **NO** on the right. Say several one syllable words. Have the student point to the word **YES** if the word is part of the targeted word family and **NO** if it is not. Have student repeat each word that is part of the word family. Continue saying one-syllable words until the student can confidently identify the words that are part of the targeted word family without hesitation.

STEP FOUR: Explain to student that words that are part of the same word family are called **rhyming** words. Say two words (one of which is a member of the targeted word family) and have the student say whether or not they rhyme. Continue saying pairs of words and have the student say YES if they rhyme and NO if they don't rhyme.

STEP FIVE: Repeat steps two, three, and four with the word families *-eft, -elt, -est, -ust,* and *-ass*.

STEP SIX: Assess the student to ascertain whether or not mastery of this lesson has been achieved. Follow the assessment directions and record the results on the 'Rhyming and Word Families Mini-Assessments Recording Sheet'. If the student has mastered this lesson, move on to the next lesson. If the student has NOT mastered this lesson, repeat lesson until mastery has been obtained.

<u>TEACHING TO MASTERY IS THE GOAL</u>

Rhyming and Word Families: Lesson 12

Lesson Name: Hearing More Words that Rhyme *-amp, -iss, -oss, -omp, -ess, -ump*

Description of Lesson/Activity: Through repeated exposure to rhyming words, the student identifies words that are from the same word family.

Procedures for Implementing the Activity:

STEP ONE: <u>Briefly</u> review with student basic letter recognition and letter sounds skills. Have the student state the **name and sounds** of letters or blends as you point to them using a letter or blends chart. Explain to student that letters go together to form words and that many words belong to families. Explain that words who come from the same family all sound alike because their ending sounds match. Explain that today he/she will learn words from six different word families.

STEP TWO: Show the student the letters 'amp' (using magnetic letters, foam letters, letter cards, paper-pencil, etc.). Have student say the sounds for all of the letters. Say the letters blended together and have the student repeat. Tell the student that there are many words that end with the 'amp' sound. Say several 'amp' family words by putting both single consonants and consonant blends in front of the sound. Point to the letters on display in front of the student as each word is pronounced.

STEP THREE: On a piece of paper write the word **YES** on the left side and **NO** on the right. Say several one syllable words. Have the student point to the word **YES** if the word is part of the targeted word family and **NO** if it is not. Have student repeat each word that is part of the word family. Continue saying one-syllable words until the student can confidently identify the words that are part of the targeted word family without hesitation.

STEP FOUR: Explain to student that words that are part of the same word family are called **rhyming** words. Say two words (one of which is a member of the targeted word family) and have the student say whether or not they rhyme. Continue saying pairs of words and have the student say YES if they rhyme and NO if they don't rhyme.

STEP FIVE: Repeat steps two, three, and four with the word families , *-iss, -oss, -omp, -ess,* and *-ump*

STEP SIX: Assess the student to ascertain whether or not mastery of this lesson has been achieved. Follow the assessment directions and record the results on the 'Rhyming and Word Families Mini-Assessments Recording Sheet'. If the student has mastered this lesson, move on to the next lesson. If the student has NOT mastered this lesson, repeat lesson until mastery has been obtained.

<u>TEACHING TO MASTERY IS THE GOAL</u>

Rhyming and Word Families: Lesson 13

Lesson Name: Saying More Words that Rhyme -all, -alm, -ill, -old, -oll, -ell, -elp, -ull, -and, -ang, -ank, -ing, -ink, -int, -ond, -ong, -end, -ung, -unk, -ant, -art, -ast, -ift, -irt, -ist, -ort, -ost, -eft, -elt, -est, -ust, -ass, -amp, -iss, -oss, -omp, -ess, -ump

Description of Lesson/Activity: Through repeated exposure to word family words, the student orally states pairs of words that rhyme.

Procedures for Implementing the Activity:
STEP ONE: Explain to student that today he/she will practice saying rhyming words. Tell the student that he/she will say words from the word families learned in lessons 6-12.

STEP TWO: On a piece of paper (or using letter cards, tiles, etc.) write one of the word endings focused on in lessons 6-12. Pronounce the word family and have the student repeat.

STEP THREE: Model for the student how you can say two words from that word family that rhyme. First, say the word ending. Next say one word from that family. Then say another word from that family. Finally restate the word ending. (Example: "all" ... "fall" ... "tall" ... "all")

STEP FOUR: Explain to student that he/she will do the same with other word families. Assist the student when he/she has trouble thinking of words that rhyme. Spend AMPLE time on this step to ensure the student has a firm grasp on the concept of rhyming.

STEP FIVE: Assess the student to ascertain whether or not mastery of this lesson has been achieved. Follow the assessment directions and record the results on the 'Rhyming and Word Families Mini-Assessments Recording Sheet'. If the student has mastered this lesson, move on to the next lesson. If the student has NOT mastered this lesson, repeat lesson until mastery has been obtained.

<u>TEACHING TO MASTERY IS THE GOAL</u>

Rhyming and Word Families: Lesson 14

Lesson Name: Hearing Even More Words that Rhyme *-ash, -ath, -atch, -arch, -ish, -ith*

Description of Lesson/Activity: Through repeated exposure to rhyming words, the student identifies words that are from the same word family.

Procedures for Implementing the Activity:

STEP ONE: <u>Briefly</u> review with student basic letter recognition and letter sounds skills. Have the student state the **name and sounds** of letters or blends as you point to them using a letter or blends chart. Explain to student that letters go together to form words and that many words belong to families. Explain that words who come from the same family all sound alike because their ending sounds match. Explain that today he/she will learn words from six different word families.

STEP TWO: Show the student the letters 'ash' (using magnetic letters, foam letters, letter cards, paper-pencil, etc.). Have student say the sounds for all of the letters. Say the letters blended together and have the student repeat. Tell the student that there are many words that end with the 'ash' sound. Say several 'ash' family words by putting both single consonants and consonant blends in front of the sound. Point to the letters on display in front of the student as each word is pronounced.

STEP THREE: On a piece of paper write the word **YES** on the left side and **NO** on the right. Say several one syllable words. Have the student point to the word **YES** if the word is part of the targeted word family and **NO** if it is not. Have student repeat each word that is part of the word family. Continue saying one-syllable words until the student can confidently identify the words that are part of the targeted word family without hesitation.

STEP FOUR: Explain to student that words that are part of the same word family are called **rhyming** words. Say two words (one of which is a member of the targeted word family) and have the student say whether or not they rhyme. Continue saying pairs of words and have the student say YES if they rhyme and NO if they don't rhyme.

STEP FIVE: Repeat steps two, three, and four with the word families *-ath, -atch, -arch, -ish,* and *-ith.*

STEP SIX: Assess the student to ascertain whether or not mastery of this lesson has been achieved. Follow the assessment directions and record the results on the 'Rhyming and Word Families Mini-Assessments Recording Sheet'. If the student has mastered this lesson, move on to the next lesson. If the student has NOT mastered this lesson, repeat lesson until mastery has been obtained.

<u>TEACHING TO MASTERY IS THE GOAL</u>

Rhyming and Word Families: Lesson 15

Lesson Name: Hearing Even More Words that Rhyme *-itch, -irth, -osh, -otch, -oth, -orch*

Description of Lesson/Activity: Through repeated exposure to rhyming words, the student identifies words that are from the same word family.

Procedures for Implementing the Activity:

STEP ONE: <u>Briefly</u> review with student basic letter recognition and letter sounds skills. Have the student state the **name and sounds** of letters or blends as you point to them using a letter or blends chart. Explain to student that letters go together to form words and that many words belong to families. Explain that words who come from the same family all sound alike because their ending sounds match. Explain that today he/she will learn words from six different word families.

STEP TWO: Show the student the letters 'itch' (using magnetic letters, foam letters, letter cards, paper-pencil, etc.). Have student say the sounds for all of the letters. Say the letters blended together and have the student repeat. Tell the student that there are many words that end with the 'itch' sound. Say several 'itch' family words by putting both single consonants and consonant blends in front of the sound. Point to the letters on display in front of the student as each word is pronounced.

STEP THREE: On a piece of paper write the word **YES** on the left side and **NO** on the right. Say several one syllable words. Have the student point to the word **YES** if the word is part of the targeted word family and **NO** if it is not. Have student repeat each word that is part of the word family. Continue saying one-syllable words until the student can confidently identify the words that are part of the targeted word family without hesitation.

STEP FOUR: Explain to student that words that are part of the same word family are called **rhyming** words. Say two words (one of which is a member of the targeted word family) and have the student say whether or not they rhyme. Continue saying pairs of words and have the student say YES if they rhyme and NO if they don't rhyme.

STEP FIVE: Repeat steps two, three, and four with the word families *-irth, -osh, -otch, -oth,* and *-orch.*

STEP SIX: Assess the student to ascertain whether or not mastery of this lesson has been achieved. Follow the assessment directions and record the results on the 'Rhyming and Word Families Mini-Assessments Recording Sheet'. If the student has mastered this lesson, move on to the next lesson. If the student has NOT mastered this lesson, repeat lesson until mastery has been obtained.

<u>TEACHING TO MASTERY IS THE GOAL</u>

Rhyming and Word Families: Lesson 16

Lesson Name: Hearing Long Vowel Rhyming Words *-ace, -ade, -age, -ake, -ale, -ame, -ape*

Description of Lesson/Activity: Through repeated exposure to rhyming words, the student identifies words that are from the same word family.

Procedures for Implementing the Activity:

STEP ONE: <u>Briefly</u> review with student basic letter recognition and letter sounds skills. Have the student state the **name and sounds** of letters or blends as you point to them using a letter or blends chart. Explain to student that letters go together to form words and that many words belong to families. Explain that words who come from the same family all sound alike because their ending sounds match. Explain that today he/she will learn words from seven different word families.

STEP TWO: Show the student the letters 'ace' (using magnetic letters, foam letters, letter cards, paper-pencil, etc.). Have student say the sounds for all of the letters using a long vowel sound. Say the letters blended together and have the student repeat. Tell the student that there are many words that end with the 'ace' sound. Say several 'ace' family words by putting both single consonants and consonant blends in front of the sound. Point to the letters on display in front of the student as each word is pronounced.

STEP THREE: On a piece of paper write the word **YES** on the left side and **NO** on the right. Say several one syllable words. Have the student point to the word **YES** if the word is part of the targeted word family and **NO** if it is not. Have student repeat each word that is part of the word family. Continue saying one-syllable words until the student can confidently identify the words that are part of the targeted word family without hesitation.

STEP FOUR: Explain to student that words that are part of the same word family are called **rhyming** words. Say two words (one of which is a member of the targeted word family) and have the student say whether or not they rhyme. Continue saying pairs of words and have the student say YES if they rhyme and NO if they don't rhyme.

STEP FIVE: Repeat steps two, three, and four with the word families *-ade, -age, -ake, -ale, -ame,* and *–ape.*

STEP SIX: Assess the student to ascertain whether or not mastery of this lesson has been achieved. Follow the assessment directions and record the results on the 'Rhyming and Word Families Mini-Assessments Recording Sheet'. If the student has mastered this lesson, move on to the next lesson. If the student has NOT mastered this lesson, repeat lesson until mastery has been obtained.

<u>TEACHING TO MASTERY IS THE GOAL</u>

Rhyming and Word Families: Lesson 17

Lesson Name: Hearing Long Vowel Rhyming Words *-ate, -ice, -ide, -ife, -ile, -ine, -ite*

Description of Lesson/Activity: Through repeated exposure to rhyming words, the student identifies words that are from the same word family.

Procedures for Implementing the Activity:
STEP ONE: Briefly review with student basic letter recognition and letter sounds skills. Have the student state the **name and sounds** of letters or blends as you point to them using a letter or blends chart. Explain to student that letters go together to form words and that many words belong to families. Explain that words who come from the same family all sound alike because their ending sounds match. Explain that today he/she will learn words from seven different word families.

STEP TWO: Show the student the letters 'ate' (using magnetic letters, foam letters, letter cards, paper-pencil, etc.). Have student say the sounds for all of the letters using a long vowel sound. Say the letters blended together and have the student repeat. Tell the student that there are many words that end with the 'ate' sound. Say several 'ate' family words by putting both single consonants and consonant blends in front of the sound. Point to the letters on display in front of the student as each word is pronounced.

STEP THREE: On a piece of paper write the word **YES** on the left side and **NO** on the right. Say several one syllable words. Have the student point to the word **YES** if the word is part of the targeted word family and **NO** if it is not. Have student repeat each word that is part of the word family. Continue saying one-syllable words until the student can confidently identify the words that are part of the targeted word family without hesitation.

STEP FOUR: Explain to student that words that are part of the same word family are called **rhyming** words. Say two words (one of which is a member of the targeted word family) and have the student say whether or not they rhyme. Continue saying pairs of words and have the student say YES if they rhyme and NO if they don't rhyme.

STEP FIVE: Repeat steps two, three, and four with the word families *-ice, -ide, -ife, -ile, -ine,* and *-ite.*

STEP SIX: Assess the student to ascertain whether or not mastery of this lesson has been achieved. Follow the assessment directions and record the results on the 'Rhyming and Word Families Mini-Assessments Recording Sheet'. If the student has mastered this lesson, move on to the next lesson. If the student has NOT mastered this lesson, repeat lesson until mastery has been obtained.

<u>TEACHING TO MASTERY IS THE GOAL</u>

Rhyming and Word Families: Lesson 18

Lesson Name: Hearing Long Vowel Rhyming Words *-ive, -ode, -oke, -ole, -one, -ope, -ote*

Description of Lesson/Activity: Through repeated exposure to rhyming words, the student identifies words that are from the same word family.

Procedures for Implementing the Activity:
STEP ONE: Briefly review with student basic letter recognition and letter sounds skills. Have the student state the **name and sounds** of letters or blends as you point to them using a letter or blends chart. Explain to student that letters go together to form words and that many words belong to families. Explain that words who come from the same family all sound alike because their ending sounds match. Explain that today he/she will learn words from seven different word families.

STEP TWO: Show the student the letters 'ive' (using magnetic letters, foam letters, letter cards, paper-pencil, etc.). Have student say the sounds for all of the letters using a long vowel sound. Say the letters blended together and have the student repeat. Tell the student that there are many words that end with the 'ive' sound. Say several 'ive' family words by putting both single consonants and consonant blends in front of the sound. Point to the letters on display in front of the student as each word is pronounced.

STEP THREE: On a piece of paper write the word **YES** on the left side and **NO** on the right. Say several one syllable words. Have the student point to the word **YES** if the word is part of the targeted word family and **NO** if it is not. Have student repeat each word that is part of the word family. Continue saying one-syllable words until the student can confidently identify the words that are part of the targeted word family without hesitation.

STEP FOUR: Explain to student that words that are part of the same word family are called **rhyming** words. Say two words (one of which is a member of the targeted word family) and have the student say whether or not they rhyme. Continue saying pairs of words and have the student say YES if they rhyme and NO if they don't rhyme.

STEP FIVE: Repeat steps two, three, and four with the word families *-ode, -oke, -ole, -one, -ope,* and *-ote.*

STEP SIX: Assess the student to ascertain whether or not mastery of this lesson has been achieved. Follow the assessment directions and record the results on the 'Rhyming and Word Families Mini-Assessments Recording Sheet'. If the student has mastered this lesson, move on to the next lesson. If the student has NOT mastered this lesson, repeat lesson until mastery has been obtained.

TEACHING TO MASTERY IS THE GOAL

Rhyming and Word Families: Lesson 19

Lesson Name: Hearing <u>Special</u> Long Vowel Rhyming Words *-aid, -ail, -ain, -ait, -ay, -eat, -each*

Description of Lesson/Activity: Through repeated exposure to rhyming words, the student identifies words that are from the same word family.

Procedures for Implementing the Activity:
STEP ONE: <u>Briefly</u> review with student basic letter recognition and letter sounds skills. Have the student state the **name and sounds** of letters or blends as you point to them using a letter or blends chart. Explain to student that letters go together to form words and that many words belong to families. Explain that words who come from the same family all sound alike because their ending sounds match. Explain that today he/she will learn words from seven different word families.

STEP TWO: Show the student the letters 'aid' (using magnetic letters, foam letters, letter cards, paper-pencil, etc.). Explain that this word family is special because it has two vowels next to each other. Also explain that in these words, only the first vowel makes a sound while the other vowel is remains silent. Pronounce the word ending 'aid' paying close attention to the first vowel saying its name. Tell the student that there are many words that end with the 'aid' sound. Say several 'aid' family words by putting both single consonants and consonant blends in front of the sound. Point to the letters on display in front of the student as each word is pronounced.

STEP THREE: On a piece of paper write the word **YES** on the left side and **NO** on the right. Say several one syllable words. Have the student point to the word **YES** if the word is part of the targeted word family and **NO** if it is not. Have student repeat each word that is part of the word family. Continue saying one-syllable words until the student can confidently identify the words that are part of the targeted word family without hesitation.

STEP FOUR: Explain to student that words that are part of the same word family are called **rhyming** words. Say two words (one of which is a member of the targeted word family) and have the student say whether or not they rhyme. Continue saying pairs of words and have the student say YES if they rhyme and NO if they don't rhyme.

STEP FIVE: Repeat steps two, three, and four with the word families *-ail, -ain, -ait, -ay, -eat,* and *-each.*

STEP SIX: Assess the student to ascertain whether or not mastery of this lesson has been achieved. Follow the assessment directions and record the results on the 'Rhyming and Word Families Mini-Assessments Recording Sheet'. If the student has mastered this lesson, move on to the next lesson. If the student has NOT mastered this lesson, repeat lesson until mastery has been obtained.

<u>TEACHING TO MASTERY IS THE GOAL</u>

Rhyming and Word Families: Lesson 20

Lesson Name: Hearing <u>Special</u> Long Vowel Rhyming Words *-ead, -eak, -eam, -ean, -eet, -eed, -eek*

Description of Lesson/Activity: Through repeated exposure to rhyming words, the student identifies words that are from the same word family.

Procedures for Implementing the Activity:
STEP ONE: <u>Briefly</u> review with student basic letter recognition and letter sounds skills. Have the student state the **name and sounds** of letters or blends as you point to them using a letter or blends chart. Explain to student that letters go together to form words and that many words belong to families. Explain that words who come from the same family all sound alike because their ending sounds match. Explain that today he/she will learn words from seven different word families.

STEP TWO: Show the student the letters 'ead' (using magnetic letters, foam letters, letter cards, paper-pencil, etc.). Explain that this word family is special because it has two vowels next to each other. Also explain that in these words, only the first vowel makes a sound while the other vowel is remains silent. Pronounce the word ending 'ead' paying close attention to the first vowel saying its name. Tell the student that there are many words that end with the 'ead' sound. Say several 'ead' family words by putting both single consonants and consonant blends in front of the sound. Point to the letters on display in front of the student as each word is pronounced.

STEP THREE: On a piece of paper write the word **YES** on the left side and **NO** on the right. Say several one syllable words. Have the student point to the word **YES** if the word is part of the targeted word family and **NO** if it is not. Have student repeat each word that is part of the word family. Continue saying one-syllable words until the student can confidently identify the words that are part of the targeted word family without hesitation.

STEP FOUR: Explain to student that words that are part of the same word family are called **rhyming** words. Say two words (one of which is a member of the targeted word family) and have the student say whether or not they rhyme. Continue saying pairs of words and have the student say YES if they rhyme and NO if they don't rhyme.

STEP FIVE: Repeat steps two, three, and four with the word families *-eak, -eam, -ean, -eet, -eed,* and *-eek*.

STEP SIX: Assess the student to ascertain whether or not mastery of this lesson has been achieved. Follow the assessment directions and record the results on the 'Rhyming and Word Families Mini-Assessments Recording Sheet'. If the student has mastered this lesson, move on to the next lesson. If the student has NOT mastered this lesson, repeat lesson until mastery has been obtained.

<u>TEACHING TO MASTERY IS THE GOAL</u>

Rhyming and Word Families: Lesson 21

Lesson Name: Hearing <u>Special</u> Long Vowel Rhyming Words *-eel, -eem, -eep, -oach, -oad, -oam, -oan, oat*

Description of Lesson/Activity: Through repeated exposure to rhyming words, the student identifies words that are from the same word family.

Procedures for Implementing the Activity:
STEP ONE: <u>Briefly</u> review with student basic letter recognition and letter sounds skills. Have the student state the **name and sounds** of letters or blends as you point to them using a letter or blends chart. Explain to student that letters go together to form words and that many words belong to families. Explain that words who come from the same family all sound alike because their ending sounds match. Explain that today he/she will learn words from seven different word families.

STEP TWO: Show the student the letters 'eel' (using magnetic letters, foam letters, letter cards, paper-pencil, etc.). Explain that this word family is special because it has two vowels next to each other. Also explain that in these words, only the first vowel makes a sound while the other vowel is remains silent. Pronounce the word ending 'eel' paying close attention to the first vowel saying its name. Tell the student that there are many words that end with the 'eel' sound. Say several 'eel' family words by putting both single consonants and consonant blends in front of the sound. Point to the letters on display in front of the student as each word is pronounced.

STEP THREE: On a piece of paper write the word **YES** on the left side and **NO** on the right. Say several one syllable words. Have the student point to the word **YES** if the word is part of the targeted word family and **NO** if it is not. Have student repeat each word that is part of the word family. Continue saying one-syllable words until the student can confidently identify the words that are part of the targeted word family without hesitation.

STEP FOUR: Explain to student that words that are part of the same word family are called **rhyming** words. Say two words (one of which is a member of the targeted word family) and have the student say whether or not they rhyme. Continue saying pairs of words and have the student say YES if they rhyme and NO if they don't rhyme.

STEP FIVE: Repeat steps two, three, and four with the word families *-eem, -eep, -oach, -oad, -oam, -oan,* and *-oat.*

STEP SIX: Assess the student to ascertain whether or not mastery of this lesson has been achieved. Follow the assessment directions and record the results on the 'Rhyming and Word Families Mini-Assessments Recording Sheet'. If the student has mastered this lesson, move on to the next lesson. If the student has NOT mastered this lesson, repeat lesson until mastery has been obtained.
<u>TEACHING TO MASTERY IS THE GOAL</u>

Rhyming and Word Families: Lesson 22

Lesson Name: Saying Even More Words that Rhyme -ash, -ath, -atch, -arch, -ish, -ith, -itch, -irth, -osh, -otch, -oth, -orch, -ace, -ade, -age, -ake, -ale, -ame, -ape, -ate, -ice, -ide, -ife, -ile, -ine, -ite, -ive, -ode, -oke, -ole, -one, -ope, -ote, -aid, -ail, -ain, -ait, -ay, -eat, -each, -ead, -eak, -eam, -ean, -eet, -eed, -eek, -eel, -eem, -eep, -oach, -oad, -oam, -oan, -oat

Description of Lesson/Activity: Through repeated exposure to word family words, the student orally states pairs of words that rhyme.

Procedures for Implementing the Activity:
STEP ONE: Explain to student that today he/she will practice saying rhyming words. Tell the student that he/she will say words from the word families learned in lessons 14-21.

STEP TWO: On a piece of paper (or using letter cards, tiles, etc.) write one of the word endings focused on in lessons 14-21. Pronounce the word family and have the student repeat.

STEP THREE: Model for the student how you can say two words from that word family that rhyme. First, say the word ending. Next say one word from that family. Then say another word from that family. Finally restate the word ending. (Example: "ash" … "bash" … "trash" … ash")

STEP FOUR: Explain to student that he/she will do the same with other word families. Assist the student when he/she has trouble thinking of words that rhyme. Spend AMPLE time on this step to ensure the student has a firm grasp on the concept of rhyming.

STEP FIVE: Assess the student to ascertain whether or not mastery of this lesson has been achieved. Follow the assessment directions and record the results on the 'Rhyming and Word Families Mini-Assessments Recording Sheet'. If the student has mastered this lesson, move on to the next lesson. If the student has NOT mastered this lesson, repeat lesson until mastery has been obtained.

<u>TEACHING TO MASTERY IS THE GOAL</u>

Rhyming and Word Families: Lesson 23

Lesson Name: Hearing Special Rhyming Words *-oil, -oin, -oint, -oist, -oot, -ook, -oom*

Description of Lesson/Activity: Through repeated exposure to rhyming words, the student identifies words that are from the same word family.

Procedures for Implementing the Activity:

STEP ONE: <u>Briefly</u> review with student basic letter recognition and letter sounds skills. Have the student state the **name and sounds** of letters or blends as you point to them using a letter or blends chart. Explain to student that letters go together to form words and that many words belong to families. Explain that words who come from the same family all sound alike because their ending sounds match. Explain that today he/she will learn words from seven different word families.

STEP TWO: Show the student the letters 'oil' (using magnetic letters, foam letters, letter cards, paper-pencil, etc.). Explain that this word family is special because the vowels make a special sound. Explain that in these words, the vowel combination of /oi/ makes the /oi/ sound (as the 'oy' sound in 'boy'). Pronounce the word ending 'oil' paying close attention to the /oi/ sound. Tell the student that there are many words that end with the 'oil' sound. Say several 'oil' family words by putting both single consonants and consonant blends in front of the sound. Point to the letters on display in front of the student as each word is pronounced.

STEP THREE: On a piece of paper write the word **YES** on the left side and **NO** on the right. Say several one syllable words. Have the student point to the word **YES** if the word is part of the targeted word family and **NO** if it is not. Have student repeat each word that is part of the word family. Continue saying one-syllable words until the student can confidently identify the words that are part of the targeted word family without hesitation.

STEP FOUR: Explain to student that words that are part of the same word family are called **rhyming** words. Say two words (one of which is a member of the targeted word family) and have the student say whether or not they rhyme. Continue saying pairs of words and have the student say YES if they rhyme and NO if they don't rhyme.

STEP FIVE: Repeat steps two, three, and four with the word families *-oin, -oint, -oist, -oot, -ook,* and *-oom.* **Special Note:** When working with the -oot, -ook, and -oom sounds be sure to focus on those special sounds. The rhyming lessons in this chapter are designed to train the student's ears and not teach specific phonics rules. However, it is advisable to inform the student that several word family words do not follow the same rules that many of the other words do.

STEP SIX: Assess the student to ascertain whether or not mastery of this lesson has been achieved. Follow the assessment directions and record the results on the 'Rhyming and Word Families Mini-Assessments Recording Sheet'. If the student has mastered this lesson, move on to the next lesson. If the student has NOT mastered this lesson, repeat lesson until mastery has been obtained.
<u>TEACHING TO MASTERY IS THE GOAL</u>

Rhyming and Word Families: Lesson 24

Lesson Name: Hearing Special Rhyming Words *-ound, -our, -ouse, -out, -oon, -oop*

Description of Lesson/Activity: Through repeated exposure to rhyming words, the student identifies words that are from the same word family.

Procedures for Implementing the Activity:

STEP ONE: Briefly review with student basic letter recognition and letter sounds skills. Have the student state the **name and sounds** of letters or blends as you point to them using a letter or blends chart. Explain to student that letters go together to form words and that many words belong to families. Explain that words who come from the same family all sound alike because their ending sounds match. Explain that today he/she will learn words from seven different word families.

STEP TWO: Show the student the letters 'ound' (using magnetic letters, foam letters, letter cards, paper-pencil, etc.). Explain that this word family is special because the vowels make a special sound. Explain that in these words, the vowel combination of 'ou' makes the /ou/ sound (the same sound we say when we are in pain). Pronounce the word ending 'ound' paying close attention to the /ou/ sound. Tell the student that there are many words that end with the 'ound' sound. Say several 'ound' family words by putting both single consonants and consonant blends in front of the sound. Point to the letters on display in front of the student as each word is pronounced.

STEP THREE: On a piece of paper write the word **YES** on the left side and **NO** on the right. Say several one syllable words. Have the student point to the word **YES** if the word is part of the targeted word family and **NO** if it is not. Have student repeat each word that is part of the word family. Continue saying one-syllable words until the student can confidently identify the words that are part of the targeted word family without hesitation.

STEP FOUR: Explain to student that words that are part of the same word family are called **rhyming** words. Say two words (one of which is a member of the targeted word family) and have the student say whether or not they rhyme. Continue saying pairs of words and have the student say YES if they rhyme and NO if they don't rhyme.

STEP FIVE: Repeat steps two, three, and four with the word families *-our, -ouse, -out, -oon,* and *-oop*. **Special Note:** When working with the -oon and -oop words, be sure to focus on those special sounds. The rhyming lessons in this chapter are designed to train the student's ears and not teach specific phonics rules. However, it is advisable to inform the student that several word family words do not follow the same rules that many of the other words do.

STEP SIX: Assess the student to ascertain whether or not mastery of this lesson has been achieved. Follow the assessment directions and record the results on the 'Rhyming and Word Families Mini-Assessments Recording Sheet'. If the student has mastered this lesson, move on to the next lesson. If the student has NOT mastered this lesson, repeat lesson until mastery has been obtained.

TEACHING TO MASTERY IS THE GOAL

Rhyming and Word Families: Lesson 25

Lesson Name: Hearing Special r-Controlled Rhyming Words *-ar, -ard, -arm, -arn, -art, -er, -ern*

Description of Lesson/Activity: Through repeated exposure to rhyming words, the student identifies words that are from the same word family.

Procedures for Implementing the Activity:
STEP ONE: Briefly review with student basic letter recognition and letter sounds skills. Have the student state the **name and sounds** of letters or blends as you point to them using a letter or blends chart. Explain to student that letters go together to form words and that many words belong to families. Explain that words who come from the same family all sound alike because their ending sounds match. Explain that today he/she will learn words from seven different word families.

STEP TWO: Show the student the letters 'ar' (using magnetic letters, foam letters, letter cards, paper-pencil, etc.). Explain that this word family is special because the letter 'r' controls what the vowel says. Explain that in these words, the 'ar' sound says the /ar/ sound (as in the sound that pirates make). Pronounce the word ending 'ar' paying close attention to the /ar/ sound. Tell the student that there are many words that end with the 'ar' sound. Say several 'ar' family words by putting both single consonants and consonant blends in front of the sound. Point to the letters on display in front of the student as each word is pronounced.

STEP THREE: On a piece of paper write the word **YES** on the left side and **NO** on the right. Say several one syllable words. Have the student point to the word **YES** if the word is part of the targeted word family and **NO** if it is not. Have student repeat each word that is part of the word family. Continue saying one-syllable words until the student can confidently identify the words that are part of the targeted word family without hesitation.

STEP FOUR: Explain to student that words that are part of the same word family are called **rhyming** words. Say two words (one of which is a member of the targeted word family) and have the student say whether or not they rhyme. Continue saying pairs of words and have the student say YES if they rhyme and NO if they don't rhyme.

STEP FIVE: Repeat steps two, three, and four with the word families *-ard, -arm, -arn, -art, -er,* and *-ern*

STEP SIX: Assess the student to ascertain whether or not mastery of this lesson has been achieved. Follow the assessment directions and record the results on the 'Rhyming and Word Families Mini-Assessments Recording Sheet'. If the student has mastered this lesson, move on to the next lesson. If the student has NOT mastered this lesson, repeat lesson until mastery has been obtained.

<u>TEACHING TO MASTERY IS THE GOAL</u>

Rhyming and Word Families: Lesson 26

<u>Lesson Name:</u> Hearing Special r-Controlled Rhyming Words *-ird, -irt, -or, -ord, -ork, -orn, -ir, -ur*

<u>Description of Lesson/Activity</u>: Through repeated exposure to rhyming words, the student identifies words that are from the same word family.

<u>Procedures for Implementing the Activity</u>:

STEP ONE: <u>Briefly</u> review with student basic letter recognition and letter sounds skills. Have the student state the **name and sounds** of letters or blends as you point to them using a letter or blends chart. Explain to student that letters go together to form words and that many words belong to families. Explain that words who come from the same family all sound alike because their ending sounds match. Explain that today he/she will learn words from seven different word families.

STEP TWO: Show the student the letters 'ird' (using magnetic letters, foam letters, letter cards, paper-pencil, etc.). Explain that this word family is special because the letter 'r' controls what the vowel says. Explain that in these words, the 'ird' sound says the /ird/ sound (as in the word 'bird'). Pronounce the word ending 'ird' paying close attention to the /ird/ sound. Tell the student that there are many words that end with the 'ird' sound. Say several 'ird' family words by putting both single consonants and consonant blends in front of the sound. Point to the letters on display in front of the student as each word is pronounced.

STEP THREE: On a piece of paper write the word **YES** on the left side and **NO** on the right. Say several one syllable words. Have the student point to the word **YES** if the word is part of the targeted word family and **NO** if it is not. Have student repeat each word that is part of the word family. Continue saying one-syllable words until the student can confidently identify the words that are part of the targeted word family without hesitation.

STEP FOUR: Explain to student that words that are part of the same word family are called **rhyming** words. Say two words (one of which is a member of the targeted word family) and have the student say whether or not they rhyme. Continue saying pairs of words and have the student say YES if they rhyme and NO if they don't rhyme.

STEP FIVE: Repeat steps two, three, and four with the word families *-irt, -or, -ord, -ork, -orn, -ir,* and *-ur.*

STEP SIX: Assess the student to ascertain whether or not mastery of this lesson has been achieved. Follow the assessment directions and record the results on the 'Rhyming and Word Families Mini-Assessments Recording Sheet'. If the student has mastered this lesson, move on to the next lesson. If the student has NOT mastered this lesson, repeat lesson until mastery has been obtained.

<u>TEACHING TO MASTERY IS THE GOAL</u>

Rhyming and Word Families: Lesson 27

Lesson Name: Hearing Special l-Controlled Rhyming Words *-ald, -alk, -eld, -elt, -ild, -old*

Description of Lesson/Activity: Through repeated exposure to rhyming words, the student identifies words that are from the same word family.

Procedures for Implementing the Activity:

STEP ONE: <u>Briefly</u> review with student basic letter recognition and letter sounds skills. Have the student state the **name and sounds** of letters or blends as you point to them using a letter or blends chart. Explain to student that letters go together to form words and that many words belong to families. Explain that words who come from the same family all sound alike because their ending sounds match. Explain that today he/she will learn words from seven different word families.

STEP TWO: Show the student the letters 'ald' (using magnetic letters, foam letters, letter cards, paper-pencil, etc.). Explain that this word family is special because the letter 'l' controls what the vowel says. Pronounce the word ending 'ald' paying close attention to the /ald/ sound. Tell the student that there are many words that end with the 'ald' sound. Say several 'ald' family words by putting both single consonants and consonant blends in front of the sound. Point to the letters on display in front of the student as each word is pronounced.

STEP THREE: On a piece of paper write the word **YES** on the left side and **NO** on the right. Say several one syllable words. Have the student point to the word **YES** if the word is part of the targeted word family and **NO** if it is not. Have student repeat each word that is part of the word family. Continue saying one-syllable words until the student can confidently identify the words that are part of the targeted word family without hesitation.

STEP FOUR: Explain to student that words that are part of the same word family are called **rhyming** words. Say two words (one of which is a member of the targeted word family) and have the student say whether or not they rhyme. Continue saying pairs of words and have the student say YES if they rhyme and NO if they don't rhyme.

STEP FIVE: Repeat steps two, three, and four with the word families *-alk, -eld, -elt, -ild,* and *-old*

STEP SIX: Assess the student to ascertain whether or not mastery of this lesson has been achieved. Follow the assessment directions and record the results on the 'Rhyming and Word Families Mini-Assessments Recording Sheet'. If the student has mastered this lesson, move on to the next lesson. If the student has NOT mastered this lesson, repeat lesson until mastery has been obtained.

<u>TEACHING TO MASTERY IS THE GOAL</u>

Rhyming and Word Families: Lesson 28

Lesson Name: Hearing Special w-Controlled Rhyming Words *-aw, -awn, -ew, -ow, -own*

Description of Lesson/Activity: Through repeated exposure to rhyming words, the student identifies words that are from the same word family.

Procedures for Implementing the Activity:

STEP ONE: <u>Briefly</u> review with student basic letter recognition and letter sounds skills. Have the student state the **name and sounds** of letters or blends as you point to them using a letter or blends chart. Explain to student that letters go together to form words and that many words belong to families. Explain that words who come from the same family all sound alike because their ending sounds match. Explain that today he/she will learn words from seven different word families.

STEP TWO: Show the student the letters 'aw' (using magnetic letters, foam letters, letter cards, paper-pencil, etc.). Explain that this word family is special because the letter 'w' controls what the vowel says. Pronounce the word ending 'aw' paying close attention to the /aw/ sound. Tell the student that there are many words that end with the 'aw' sound. Say several 'aw' family words by putting both single consonants and consonant blends in front of the sound. Point to the letters on display in front of the student as each word is pronounced.

STEP THREE: On a piece of paper write the word **YES** on the left side and **NO** on the right. Say several one syllable words. Have the student point to the word **YES** if the word is part of the targeted word family and **NO** if it is not. Have student repeat each word that is part of the word family. Continue saying one-syllable words until the student can confidently identify the words that are part of the targeted word family without hesitation.

STEP FOUR: Explain to student that words that are part of the same word family are called **rhyming** words. Say two words (one of which is a member of the targeted word family) and have the student say whether or not they rhyme. Continue saying pairs of words and have the student say YES if they rhyme and NO if they don't rhyme.

STEP FIVE: Repeat steps two, three, and four with the word families *-awn, -ew, -ow,* and *-own*

STEP SIX: Assess the student to ascertain whether or not mastery of this lesson has been achieved. Follow the assessment directions and record the results on the 'Rhyming and Word Families Mini-Assessments Recording Sheet'. If the student has mastered this lesson, move on to the next lesson. If the student has NOT mastered this lesson, repeat lesson until mastery has been obtained.

<u>TEACHING TO MASTERY IS THE GOAL</u>

Rhyming and Word Families: Lesson 29

Lesson Name: Saying Even More Words that Rhyme -oil, -oin, -oint, -oist, -oot, -ook, -oom, -ound, -our, -ouse, -out, -oon, -oop, -ar, -ard, -arm, -arn, -art, -er, -ern, -ird, -irt, -or, -ord, -ork, -orn, -ir, -ur, -ald, -alk, -eld, -elt, -ild, -old, -aw, -awn, -ew, -ow, -own

Description of Lesson/Activity: Through repeated exposure to word family words, the student orally states pairs of words that rhyme.

Procedures for Implementing the Activity:

STEP ONE: Explain to student that today he/she will practice saying rhyming words. Tell the student that he/she will say words from the word families learned in lessons 23-28.

STEP TWO: On a piece of paper (or using letter cards, tiles, etc.) write one of the word endings focused on in lessons 23-28. Pronounce the word family and have the student repeat.

STEP THREE: Model for the student how you can say two words from that word family that rhyme. First, say the word ending. Next say one word from that family. Then say another word from that family. Finally restate the word ending. (Example: "oil" ... "soil" ... "broil" ... "oil")

STEP FOUR: Explain to student that he/she will do the same with other word families. Assist the student when he/she has trouble thinking of words that rhyme. Spend AMPLE time on this step to ensure the student has a firm grasp on the concept of rhyming.

STEP FIVE: Assess the student to ascertain whether or not mastery of this lesson has been achieved. Follow the assessment directions and record the results on the 'Rhyming and Word Families Mini-Assessments Recording Sheet'. If the student has mastered this lesson, move on to the next lesson. If the student has NOT mastered this lesson, repeat lesson until mastery has been obtained.

<u>TEACHING TO MASTERY IS THE GOAL</u>

Rhyming and Word Families: Lesson 30

Lesson Name: Which Word Does Not Rhyme?

Description of Lesson/Activity: The student listens to three words and identifies the word that does not rhyme.

Procedures for Implementing the Activity:
STEP ONE: Review with student rhyming and word family skills. Say a word ending and have the student say at least two words that are part of that family. Continue reviewing until the student can easily say words that rhyme.

STEP TWO: Explain to student that today he/she will listen to three words and will identify the word that does *not* rhyme with the other two.

STEP THREE: Practice this skill by clearly and concisely saying three one-syllable words (two that rhyme and one that doesn't rhyme) and have the student orally state the word that doesn't rhyme.

STEP FOUR: Continue step three until the student can easily and accurately identify the word that does *not* rhyme with the other two.

STEP FIVE: Assess the student to ascertain whether or not mastery of this lesson has been achieved. Follow the assessment directions and record the results on the 'Rhyming and Word Families Mini-Assessments Recording Sheet'. If the student has mastered this lesson, move on to the next lesson. If the student has NOT mastered this lesson, repeat lesson until mastery has been obtained.

TEACHING TO MASTERY IS THE GOAL

Rhyming and Word Families: Lesson 31

Lesson Name: Rhyming and Word Families Picture Match

Description of Lesson/Activity: The student uses pictures to identify words that rhyme.

Procedures for Implementing the Activity:

STEP ONE: Review with student rhyming and word family skills. Say a word ending and have the student say at least two words that are part of that family. Continue reviewing until the student can easily say words that rhyme.

STEP TWO: Explain to student that today he/she will identify rhyming words using picture cards.

STEP THREE: Using picture cards (there are pictures included at the back of this book that may be used for this activity if you don't already have picture cards available) have the student state which of three cards rhymes with a fourth focus picture. Present the student with a row of four pictures and have him/her say the name of each. Have the student point to and say the words that rhyme with the first picture in the row.

STEP FOUR: Continue step three until the student can easily and accurately identify pictures/words that rhyme with a particular focus picture/word.

STEP FIVE: Assess the student to ascertain whether or not mastery of this lesson has been achieved. Follow the assessment directions and record the results on the 'Rhyming and Word Families Mini-Assessments Recording Sheet'. If the student has mastered this lesson, move on to the next lesson. If the student has NOT mastered this lesson, repeat lesson until mastery has been obtained.

<u>TEACHING TO MASTERY IS THE GOAL</u>

Which Pictures Rhyme with the First Picture on the Row?

Rhyming and Word Families: Lesson 32

Lesson Name: Rhyming and Word Families Final Review

Description of Lesson/Activity: The student uses pictures to identify words that rhyme.

Procedures for Implementing the Activity:

STEP ONE: Review with student rhyming and word family skills. Say a word ending and have the student say at least two words that are part of that family. Continue reviewing until the student can easily say words that rhyme.

STEP TWO: Explain to student that today he/she will identify rhyming words using picture cards.

STEP THREE: Using picture cards have the student sort cards based on their word endings. Be sure to have the student say the names of each word to ensure understanding of rhyming and word families.

STEP FOUR: Create fun ways of using the picture cards to promote mastery. For example use the cards to play "Concentration" or "Go Fish".

STEP FIVE: Assess the student to ascertain whether or not mastery of this lesson has been achieved. Follow the assessment directions and record the results on the 'Rhyming and Word Families Mini-Assessments Recording Sheet'. If the student has mastered this lesson, move on to the next lesson. If the student has NOT mastered this lesson, repeat lesson until mastery has been obtained.

TEACHING TO MASTERY IS THE GOAL

Word Family Cards

at	ad
ag	ed
en	et
ig	id

ib	og
ot	od
ub	ug
um	all

alm	ill
old	oll
ell	elp
ull	and

ang	ank
ing	ink
int	ond
ong	end

ung	unk
ant	art
ast	ift
irt	ist

ort	ost
eft	elt
est	ust
ass	amp

iss	oss
omp	ess
ump	ash
ath	atch

arch	ish
ith	itch
irth	osh
otch	oth

orch	ace
ade	age
ake	ale
ame	ape

ate	ice
ide	ife
ile	ine
ite	ive

ode	oke
ole	one
ope	ote
aid	ail

ain	ait
ay	eat
each	ead
eak	eam

ean	eet
eed	eek
eel	eem
eep	oach

oad	oam
oan	oat
oil	oin
oint	oist

oot	ook
oom	ound
our	ouse
out	oon

oop	ar
ard	arm
arn	art
er	ern

ird	irt
or	ord
ork	orn
ir	ur

ald	alk
eld	elt
ild	old
aw	awn

ew	ow
own